Sunny Side Up

Sunny Side Up

Fond Memories of Prairie Life in the 1930s

EILEEN COMSTOCK

FIFTH
HOUSE
PUBLISHERS

Front cover photograph by D. Reede / First Light
Design by Articulate Eye

The publisher gratefully acknowledges the support of The Canada Council for the Arts and the Department of Canadian Heritage. We acknowledge the financial support of the Government of Canada through the Book Publishing Industry Development Program for our publishing activities.

National Library of Canada Cataloguing in Publication Data
Comstock, Eileen, 1926-
    Sunny side up
    ISBN 1-894004-65-5
    1. Prairie Provinces—History—Anecdotes. 3. Prairie
Provinces—History—Humor. I. Title.
FC3242.9.D35C66 2001   971.2'02   C2001-911067-7
F1060.9.C66 2001

Printed in Canada.

00 01 02 03 04/ 5 4 3 2 1

First published in the United States in 2002.

Fifth House Ltd.
A Fitzhenry & Whiteside Company
1511-1800 4 St. SW
Calgary, Alberta, Canada
T2S 2S5

1-800-387-9776
www.fitzhenry.ca

To my son, Keith, and my husband, Ev, for their help,
and to the many "old-timers" who have shared these
bright spots in their memories with us all.

❖

ABOUT THE AUTHOR

EILEEN COMSTOCK grew up near Cadillac, Saskatchewan, and taught for decades in various rural schools. She has lived on the land for seventy-five years, raising children, farming, and collecting anecdotes. Her stories are broadcast regularly on CBC radio and have been collected in the popular *Aunt Mary in the Granary and Other Prairie Stories* (Fifth House, ISBN: 1-894004-54-X). She lives on a farm near Mitchellton, Saskatchewan.

TABLE OF CONTENTS

Introduction .... *ix*

Social Life in Small Towns *1*

A Mighty Fortress *13*

Good Old Golden Rule Days *21*

We Should Have a "Club" *33*

Take Me Out to the Ball Game! *43*

A Song in Our Hearts *51*

Imagination and Ingenuity *59*

Fun in the Sun ... and the Snow *69*

Fashion—Dirty Thirties Style *85*

Making Ends Meet *93*

Relief *99*

Pests, Small and Smaller *107*

Costco? I Don't Think So *119*

Bell and Marconi Were Prairie Boys at Heart ... *131*

Beyond Horsepower *137*

How to Celebrate Christmas *143*

Saving Up to Get Married *155*

Rays of Sunshine Here and There *165*

Epilogue *179*

INTRODUCTION

In the thirty years preceding the twentieth century, knowledge of the area we now know as the Prairie provinces moved from campfire legend into history books. The North-West Mounted Police marched west in 1874, bringing law and order to the Canadian frontier and driving out the fur and whiskey traders from the south who preyed on Natives, Métis, and the sparse white settlements with impartial avarice. The Canadian Pacific rail line snaked across the grasslands by 1885, uniting west and east. Surveyors tacked the border to the forty-ninth parallel with concrete posts and, with their maps, fixed corners and edges onto the wilderness.

Word spread. Homesteaders flocked in from Europe, the Mid-East, the United States, and eastern Canada. Some came for the adventure, some for freedom from oppression, but most came with the dream of having land to farm—land that they could own. Some came in groups and settled in ethnic enclaves, bringing their religion and language with them. A few, backed by family money and influence, came intending to set up their own fiefdoms where they could ride to hounds, dine and dance in style, and live the life of the gentry, supported by the labour of a cap-doffing lower class. Some envisioned a New World Utopia, their charismatic leader bringing them to a place where flags, oaths of allegiance, and military service were forever abolished.

The harsh realities of homesteading—breaking sod, digging wells, garnering fodder to over-winter livestock, building homes and barns, fighting prairie fires—could have isolated and embittered these adventurers. Oh, a few gave up and went back to the lives and worries they were more used to, but most of the immigrants adapted. Together they built schools and churches, acted as midwife to each other's births, endured hoppers and hail, and left their own work to help a neighbour stricken with illness or accident. They were no longer just Germans or Scandinavians, Russians or English, French or Ukrainians. They were Canadians— prairie people.

What makes prairie people different? For indeed we are different. We are the people who admit that the forests and mountains of the Rockies are okay—except one can't really see much, the trees and hills get in the way. We are also the people who took the co-operative idea from Rochdale, a little place in England, and ran with it until every city, town, and village had its Coop grocery, fuel company, and credit union. Seventy years ago we pooled our resources to combat robber barons on the Winnipeg Grain Exchange. We have the highest ratio of charitable donations to income in the country. And we were the fashioners of comprehensive Medicare. We thought no one should be in pain or die just because of a flat wallet.

Like the rest of the world, prairie people lived through the First World War, the flu epidemic, the stock market crash, and the Great Depression. With the depression came the decade of the "dirty thirties" on the prairies, when nature itself seemed to be the enemy. Drought and blowing dust called black winds seared souls as they seared the earth. But that is not all of the story.

In his book *Saskatchewan: A History*, Dr. John Archer wrote:

We are people who lived through the depression, the decade of the thirties. The 1929 depression affected all of Canada. The impact, apparent in the autumn, struck hard in the following winter as prices for farm produce fell, unemployment in towns and cities rose, tight money led to declining purchasing power and an atmosphere of anxiety and additional dreadful burden. The economic depression was made the more bitter by nine successive years of drought and crop failure. Impossible as it may seem, the net agricultural incomes for 1931 through 1934, and again in 1937, were reported in minus figures, a reduction in income quite unmatched in any civilized country.

The 1930s as a decade had a greater impact on Saskatchewan's people than on any other. It shaped and changed lives. In much of Canada the 1930s was the depression, but in Saskatchewan, it was the "Dirty Thirties." All the problems of drought, insect pests, erosion, low prices for produce and high winds occurred simultaneously, and continued year after year after year. By 1937 the despair of earlier days had given way to a sterner reaction and people took a kind of pride in showing the world that they could bear the worst that Nature could do to them, and laugh a little in the process.

It is the laughter that this book is about. These were strong people, good people. They were all in the same boat. They helped each other and made good things happen. They proved that it was possible to be happy in the hard times, to look at the sunny side of life when one would least expect them to.

SOCIAL LIFE IN SMALL TOWNS

In the early years of the last century great chunks of southern prairie were opened for homesteading. Most of it was broken into fields that were seeded to grain. Railroad companies, all agog with expectations of huge profits from hauling eastern manufactured goods to the hinterlands and backhauling grain, extended rail lines like tentacles out from the main lines. Soon a network of branch lines covered the area, and every seven or eight miles along the tracks a stopping place evolved. Some stops became towns, some villages, some hamlets, and a few only got to be sidings. Depending on the number of potential customers nearby, entrepreneurs set up stores and hotels, grain companies built elevators, and soon other businesses established themselves in the vicinity. In those horse-and-wagon days, most farms ended up near enough to make a return trip to "town" in one day.

By the 1930s, our little town—Cadillac, Saskatchewan—like many others on the prairie had outlived its boom. There was only one livery barn, one lumberyard, two modest grocery stores, and a meat market that was about to move its operations to a larger centre. Five grain elevators stretched out along the tracks, just east of the train station. In the middle of town the post office, several implement agencies that doubled as garages, the blacksmith shop, insurance offices, the telephone central building, the municipal office, and hardware store stood ready to serve. Two Chinese restaurants and a little laundry down a back alley were staffed by descendants of men who had been imported from China as cheap labour to lay the rails across the continent and then callously discarded when the track was done. (They were even legally barred from bringing their families to join them.) The doctor's office was in his drug store, a little cottage held an "on again, off again" beauty parlour, and the town hall, fire hall, and four churches filled up the rest of main street. On the edge of town a yellow-brick, four-room school sat next to Highway #4, with two elementary rooms on the ground floor, and two high school rooms above. I am sure there were other establishments, too, that didn't make enough of an impression on my child's mind so that I remember them as part of "town."

The town population included the people who staffed these enterprises and their families, the section hands who patrolled the rail lines, several retired couples, and a few old bachelors who manned the sidewalk benches on balmy days and took their places near the grocery store heater when the weather got rough. The male sector of the population generally maintained sort of a democratic equality based on what a man could do rather than what his name, his origin, or his accent revealed about his ancestry. However, a genteel snobbery arose among some of the town ladies who felt themselves obliged to set an example of propriety and culture for the less fortunate.

When really hard times came with the 1930s, people in towns and cities often felt it more severely than did people in rural areas. Country folk were aware of each other's situation, and there were thousands of instances where they helped one another through emergencies. Also there was usually something to eat on a farm, though it might be pretty basic. Milk, eggs, garden stuff, a chicken for the pot, all kept the wolf from the door. I can remember porridge made from ground wheat—it was pretty good! Town and city people had relied on paycheques for food, clothing, and accommodation. When paycheques were cut drastically or vanished entirely the outlook was grim. Those who ran businesses found their income starting to consist of a mix of promissory notes and bad debts. But only in the city was there enough anonymity so that a family could go hungry in dignified privacy.

In small towns like ours, times were tough, and sometimes false pride had to come down a peg or two, but nobody died for lack of food. Most of us children of the 1930s have good memories about our little towns and the people who lived in them. It was in these little towns that we first glimpsed the "other" world, the world that awaited us when we grew up.

The corner store was the mecca of each town. Ray Kains of

Southey, Saskatchewan, remembers the smells and tastes of his childhood.

There's a time in every kid's life when he is obsessed with one thing—candy. The love of my heart was a corner store—the A. Kurosky Store—grocery, dry goods, candy, and watch repairs.

It sat perched on the corner of Keats Street and Assiniboia Avenue. It had a false front and a permanent awning. A round sign in the shape of a giant pocket watch hung above the awning, boldly proclaiming WATCH REPAIR. Below it a sign simply stated A. KUROSKY.

As you entered the dimly lit confines of the store many smells greeted you. The first was the aroma of cloth and linen laid flat on long counters. Farther in you got the great smell of ginger, cinnamon, and cloves, carefully kept in bulk containers. Even the smell of fruit assailed you— sometimes a little over-ripe. On the counter sat the ever-present large round bulk cheese, wrapped in its skin of cheese cloth and carefully covered with a glass globe. Often the cheese was just a little green around the edges.

Mr. Kurosky greeted me. "Sonny, mus' be your mutter send you for some tings?"

"No, not today, Mr. Kurosky. I did a little work around town and I want to buy some candy."

"How much guilden (money) you want to spend, sonny?" he'd say with a wink. He would walk around behind the candy counter, wearing as always his buttoned-up brown sweater. It had coins in every pocket to make just the right change for you.

Once behind the counter, Mr. Kurosky went through the whole spiel. Two cents for the huge jaw breakers, the kind a kid has to take out of his mouth a hundred times in order to watch all the colour changes. One cent for a licorice pipe or cigar with little red candies on the front, so you could pretend you were smoking like the grown-ups. Five cents for a large square of fudge made by Mrs. Kurosky.

It would just melt in your mouth. Two cents for a BB bat sucker. It had a real wood stick in it—a stick you could use later on. You could carve a propeller from wood, drill a hole in the middle, insert the BB stick, give it a twirl, and you had a flying missile. Sometimes it turned out to be a misguided missile, especially if it hit your father on the head. Ten cents for a huge chunk of rabbit cheese (halva.) Mr. Kurosky gave me a small piece to taste. The initial reaction was "Yuk."

I settled on ten licorice pipes so that I would have some to share with my friend. As I contemplated my purchase, I realized that the rabbit cheese was pretty good. I would plan to buy some next time.

The preacher's son, the blacksmith's son, and the retired farmer's son often sat on the bench in front of Kurosky's store, discussing such earth-shattering things as really how long does a jaw breaker last or how best to avoid getting caught by Mr. Roth, the town constable, when we rode our bikes on the sidewalk.

The days slipped by and soon our childhood came to an end. Never again would the corner store hold the same attractions.

In the 1920s an event known as "chautauqua" spread from the eastern United States. It consisted of four or five days of amusement, drama, music, speeches, dance, and just generally good-quality entertainment, performed in large tents. Several months ahead of time, organizers would canvas the district for support. A district had to guarantee several thousand dollars worth of backing in order to book the show. As well as bringing a healthy dose of culture to the hinterland, there was an abundance of just good fun, and prairie audiences supported it wholeheartedly. The depression of the 1930s brought the whole thing to a halt, of course, but Charlie Schick of Moose Jaw, Saskatchewan, remembers one of the last performances.

The youngest of six sons is sometimes controlled by older

siblings. I was fortunate enough to have one brother who, in my opinion, never did wrong. This resulted in my doing some things I shouldn't have.

The chautauqua came to Spring Valley. Entry fee was, I think, 25 cents, which we lacked. The big tent had a considerable flap around the bottom. We studied the structure and I, the ten year old, took instructions from my twelve-year-old brother. We would roll under the flap at a point close to the front, where we had determined there were two empty seats. We would not stand up, just roll to those two front outside seats and sit down.

It worked perfectly, except that a few other kids had seen us get in. They, too, went under the flap, but then they wandered around looking for someplace to sit. They were quickly shooshed out. My brother and I sat goggle-eyed as the prestidigitator pulled endless strings of wieners and other items from the pockets of some of our young neighbours. They knew that the boys didn't have anything like that on or about them when they came in.

I don't think that the chatauqua people went broke because of our felony.

The local history book from Viceroy, Saskatchewan, contains a tale of the coming of the "real" chautauqua and a pale imitation.

In the late teens the chautauqua, a travelling variety show, was an event looked forward to by the early settlers. The show stayed for three or four days and presented afternoon and evening performances in a large tent. Many people drove for miles by horse and buggy to take in the entertainment. The introduction of radio and improved transportation did away with the necessity for such a show, but while it was going full force, travelling shows such as the "Richard Kent Stock Company" brought live theatre to the local hall.

With the coming of the 1930s and its hard times it became necessary for people to supply their own entertainment, and a community chautauqua was formed. Everyone who had any talent took part in the evening entertainment. The results ranged from excellent to "the less said about it the better." With the return of more prosperous times this was quickly forgotten.

Jean Freeman, now of Regina, Saskatchewan, was a "town kid" in the thirties. The customary Saturday night shopping trip that many farm families took to the nearest village provided an evening's enjoyment for the town kids too.

One of the happiest things we did when I was a kid in the thirties was our Saturday night treat of "watching the people go by." We were lucky because the family store was right on main street, so we could sit on our front step and watch people pass by, go shopping, visit the café (and sometimes the beer parlour!) next door, and drive up and down the street. Other people who weren't lucky enough to live on main street would fire up the family Ford and find a parking spot on main street with a good view, and then park so they could sit in comfort and "rubber-neck" as we called it. If the week had been particularly good, there would be a nickel for an ice cream cone or a "Sherbicle" (later christened "Revels"). There was always an opportunity to comment, sotto voce, about what Mrs. So-and-so was wearing, or the dreadful behaviour of those bad teenage boys who liked to climb up into the vacant store next door and throw crabapples down at passers-by, or debate about the probable cost of someone's new half-ton. In even smaller towns (like when we went to visit my grandma's village) the people-watching was enhanced because there was a night train that brought the mail, so everybody came to town to pick up their mail and see who got on and off the train. It was a great evening's entertainment, and all for free!

Jean doesn't remember the chautauquas but does reminisce about the excitement when the circus arrived in town.

In those days, the circus came to town by train, and it still had elephants to raise the tents and a torchlight parade to whet people's interest. I remember my father wrapping me in a blanket (I was probably three or four) and carrying me in his arms to watch the elephants lumbering off their train cars by torchlight and moving through the dark to raise the big top. I don't remember seeing the circus itself. We probably didn't have enough money to attend the actual show, but watching the set-up and tear-down—that magical creation and razing of a whole little city in mere hours—was great enough for a four year old. I also remember another time when Father wrapped me in blankets and carried me to the sidewalk in front of the store to watch one of the town's elevators as it burned down in a major conflagration. Another prime entertainment, absolutely free!

The town hall often doubled as a movie theatre. In our town, the only "shows" that I remember being taken to in the thirties were put on by the Saskatchewan Wheat Pool or the Department of Agriculture, and usually featured wind-ravaged farmsteads with banks of blow-dirt covered fences, abandoned farm houses with empty windows, and remnants of sand-blasted buildings leaning away from the prevailing winds. I guess the object of the show was to persuade farmers to abandon deep ploughing of summerfallow and large fields in favour of strip farming and trash cover methods that were not so susceptible to the wicked winds from the west. Anyway, admission was free, and the propaganda was usually accompanied by a ten-minute cartoon that we kids always called "The Mickey Mouse," no matter which subject was actually featured.

Jean Freeman also remembers movies.

One of the great delights in the thirties was the movies, although my own earliest experience was in 1939 when my father took me to my first movie at the old Hi-Art Theatre—*Snow White and the Seven Dwarfs*. Earlier than that, however, movies provided a welcome escape for people whose daily experiences were far from happy. In addition to the pleasure that the dramas, comedies, and adventure stories provided, there were "china nights," when everybody who attended got a piece of china. There were talent nights, when local people entertained their peers before the movie, or sometimes between reels when a captive audience was provided. And some theatres, to boost attendance, would offer "Family Nights," when whole families could attend for a set price—sometimes as little as a dime or a quarter. My father had a cousin who put the fear of God into movie-theatre owners whenever he appeared on Family Night, since he had twelve children!

In my china cabinet at this very moment is a complete setting for ten—china that my mother collected during the thirties and early forties, not from theatre-going, but by buying a particular brand of laundry detergent. I think it was Oxydol. (We all swore by Oxydol because we loved *Ma Perkins* on the radio, a soap opera that was sponsored by that brand of soap.) In every box of detergent there was a piece for your china set. There must have been thousands upon thousands of women collecting that particular pattern. But the dishes were produced in England, and part way through the campaign the war intruded, and the manufacturers had to change their plans. They switched to producing the dishes in the United States. For some reason, they were able to send over the dyes for the gilded borders on the dishes but not for the intricate centre lozenge. So some of my plates and cups and saucers, gravy boats, platters, serving dishes, demitasses, and coffee pitchers have the original design and some have a single pink rose. The dishes were proudly used on "special" occasions throughout my mother's lifetime, and now during mine, and they will pass along to my daughter when I am gone, as a reminder of a gentler, simpler time when "value added" had real meaning!

In our rural district about the only "ladies only" parties were meetings of the Lutheran Ladies Aid Society. There were usually a few men who came to them because their wives didn't drive. The men often congregated outside or in the kitchen or porch and had a good gab fest. The ladies sat in the living room, in their good dresses, each with only the very littlest of her brood to hold, or to set on the floor beside her. There was "devotion" and the business meeting and then lunch—and I am willing to bet that lunch was the best part of the meeting. Occasionally the ladies met at a "quilting bee" where they stitched or tied quilts to send to mission posts. That was usually good for a long afternoon and a lot of chatter and, of course, lunch as well.

Justine Lips (nee Dantzer), who grew up in Rush Lake, Saskatchewan, gives a good example of ladies socializing in a small town.

Social occasions that I particularly enjoyed in our town were the tea parties. Most of the time they were part of the Homemakers meetings, but sometimes one would be given to entertain a guest or to celebrate a special occasion. I used to get to help with preparations when Mother had a tea. Polishing the silver tea service was often my job. Each family had a company teapot, either china or silver, and one of the hostess's friends would be installed at the head of the table to "pour." This was a special mark of respect for the pourer. Sometimes we girls would get the job of delivering the cups of tea, always remembering to ask "cream and sugar?" of each guest.

The baking that went on before the party got to be a bit predictable with each cook having her own specialties. When someone discovered a sensational recipe it was passed around and often appeared at teas ever after. That is what happened to "Chinese Chews" and to a wonderful mouthful called "Melting Moments." Somebody introduced sandwiches made of bread rolled around canned asparagus tips with Velveeta cheese and toasted in the oven. I hardly ever see those any more. There was a similar recipe made with bread spread with undiluted cream of mushroom soup, rolled and toasted. Nothing more delicious has been invented! And there was always the Christmas cake. Some people were known for their moist rich recipes. The cake seemed to last all year. We made a big recipe and doled it out in small pieces. Somebody came up with a way of making the special Christmas cake icing using mashed potatoes, icing sugar, and almond flavouring. It really tasted a lot like the ground almond icing, which was too expensive to use all the time. And then there were pickles. We always had to have three kinds because the pickle dish had three sections. Usually they were "bread and butter," "dill," and "beet." That is until Mother decided beet pickles were too hard to handle. She had a terrible experience at a tea in Swift Current when she attempted to cut a large round beet to bite size and managed to shoot it across the room instead. She didn't see the funny side of that until long afterwards! Dad used to call our parties "Pink Teas," and I only recently discovered the origin of that name. It seems that when the Famous Five Canadian women were trying to organize a movement to have women declared "persons" so they could vote in elections, the people against the campaign would come and disrupt their meetings. They hit on the idea of having very feminine tea parties, which they called "Pink Teas," to discourage the men from attending, and were thus able to gain support for their cause. I don't know where Dad learned about Pink Teas, but certainly our Rush Lake tea parties had no political motive that I know of.

Ruth Davis and Jennie Kirkpatrick of the Mossbank area in Saskatchewan have vivid memories of the people who lived through the depression and the dances that took place in their community.

And then there were the dances! Ah, what excitement, what anticipation and preparation in readiness for those Friday night frolics. Chilled to the bone from a sleigh or

An outdoor dance at an all-day picnic near Beaverlodge, Alberta, 1933. *Glenbow Archives/NA-2923-5*

cutter ride, or a ride in the back of the friendly bachelor's old truck, still how exhilarated everyone was, upon entering the hall or the schoolhouse. The music, the merriment was infectious! Those were the days when dances were spoken for ahead of time, when the floor manager announced each dance: foxtrot, circle two-step, waltz quadrilles, squares, and so on. And who could forget the Flea Hop! The gentlemen usually clapped their hands in appreciation, but the ladies certainly did not. Who can forget: when supper partners were a symbol of popularity or a budding romance, when we danced cheek to cheek, and when the children accompanied their parents and romped or danced till they fell asleep. Oh, how fondly we remember tripping the light fantastic, even of a summer's evening in a barn loft. The popular tunes played by local talent included: "Down the River of Golden Dreams," "The Waltz You Saved for Me," "Moonlight on the River Colorado," "I Like Mountain Music," "Sweet Jennie Lee," "Old Spinning Wheel in the Parlour," "Just an Echo," "Spring Time in the Rockies," "WaHoo!" just to mention a few. There were, of course, the old traditionals: "Good

Night Sweetheart," "Home Sweet Home," and always
"God Save the King." One tune we have missed was a
great favourite of those days and so aptly says what we
have attempted in compiling this community history:

> Throw another log on the fire.
> Keep the golden memories aglow
> When our hearts were young in the springtime
> And the days of long, long ago.

(From *Furrows and Faith*, courtesy of the editor, Phyllis
Zado)

A MIGHTY FORTRESS

A s soon as the settlers had built homes for their families and shelter for their livestock, they felt the need for schools and churches. The provincial government set standards and provided loans to help establish schools, but churches were left to individual initiative. Some were built with the aid of "mission" money from churches in eastern Canada or abroad, but many groups of settlers were on their own financially. Occasionally, groups with the same ethnic and religious background got help in starting a congregation and getting a minister from their former home church, although the help did not extend to building. They worshipped wherever there was space available—often in homes or the local school—until they were able to finance building a "real" church. By the thirties, the province of Saskatchewan was dotted with little churches. A few were of brick or even stone, but most were white, clapboard-sided wooden buildings with arched windows and a little spire-topped tower over the entrance. Some towers had onion-shaped domes revealing their Orthodox roots. Some even had bell towers with slotted sides, where some day a bell might hang when the community could afford it.

Many districts were too diverse in background for any one denomination to prevail. In the Galilee area, thirty miles south of Moose Jaw, Saskatchewan, this was the case. June Mitchell remembers the influence of the church on the community.

> Sunday school and church services were a very important part of our lives, and I still see the good influence it had on some of us survivors and our descendants. For a couple of months in summer, Baptist student ministers from Ontario came and provided leadership in Sunday School and church services. They rode horseback on a second-hand

army saddle, only slightly better than bareback. Sunday morning service was in Staynor school near Cardross. Then there was a ride of over ten miles to Sugar Loaf School for an afternoon service, and then ten miles north in the evening to the little Baptist church in the Mayberry district. It is a wonder that horse and rider survived the evening service.

The rest of the year we moved from home to home for Sunday School. Houses were filled (standing room only) with all ages of people. It was non-denominational. People of many different religions attended—Greek Orthodox, Roman Catholics, Lutherans, Anglicans, Baptists, and some from the newly formed United Church of Canada. Many of us walked to the services, a few drove with horses hooked onto a wagon or "Bennett buggy," as no one around here was able to afford to keep a car running.

My own home congregation of South Immanuel Lutheran was organized in 1914 but met at homes and in the school for nearly twenty years. By 1933, although things were tough and looked to be getting tougher, the Ladies Aid had managed to save $2000 by putting on harvest suppers, auctions of handwork, quilting, and just generally putting their talents to use. (The men, who thought they ran the church, had been obliged to pay the minister with their funds, so they didn't have a nest egg.) When church construction got underway, everybody helped. Youth groups raised money for the furnace, organ, pews, pulpit, tables, and chairs. One of the congregants built the gold and white altar. The communion cup and paten were donated in memory of my grandparents. This was not an isolated incident. All over the west people were putting their faith in the land and in God to the test.

Much of the social life of the thirties centred on the church. Beth Byggdyn, of Moose Jaw, grew up near Prince Albert, in the bush area, and remembers the Sunday School picnic.

Sunday School picnics were summer highlights in my childhood. Today, the annual church outing in June usually

A gathering at a Sunday School picnic. *Beth Byggdyn*

goes by that name, but it's a far cry from what we, as children, enjoyed.

Our picnics were usually held in the grassy area of a farmer's field, not too far from the house, both to accommodate bathroom facilities (wooden outhouses) and to make it easy to fetch a needed item from the nearby home, if it hadn't been brought by the ladies who packed the picnic baskets.

One or two long tables were set up, covered with tablecloths, and the contents of the baskets were set out: fried and/or roast chicken, potato salad, jellied salads, vegetable salads, pickles, buns, pies, and cakes. There were quarts of homemade lemonade mix to be added to cold well water as needed and freezers full of rich, homemade ice cream—everything one could wish for.

Before we ate, however, races must be run. Everyone, even the married women, might participate. I don't recall that the men did. They, dressed in their Sunday best (as were their wives) complete with hats (and I have snaps to prove it!), sat and talked about the crops and things of interest to men. The picnic day was one of the few holidays enjoyed by farm folk in those days of the thirties, and they made the most of it.

The children's races always came first. Parents and older siblings helped line up the little ones and yelled encouragingly as they ran. Each was given some small prize, whether or not he/she won. As a pre-teen I enjoyed racing, the one sport in which I was any good. The married women's race [with the women racing to the finish in their Sunday clothing] looked so funny to the young woman conducting it that she rolled on the ground with laughter. There may have been a game of softball for the young adults on occasion, but it didn't comprise almost the total time spent, as it seems to do today.

The "eats" were the highlight of the picnic. One year a Swedish lady brought "rosettes" made on a special iron, and they soon disappeared, for they were a treat we seldom saw. Another year, someone brought a pot of baked beans that was so tasty that some preferred it to the ice cream. The next year baked beans appeared again, but unknown to the woman who cooked them some young rascal had laced them with a laxative so potent that a few of the enjoyers had to beat a hasty retreat into the bushes on the walk home. (Fortunately the P.A. country where I grew up was well treed.) That was the last year that baked beans appeared at our Sunday School picnic.

Avis Haug, now of Outlook, Saskatchewan, remembers that church activities were an important part of her community's social life. Her family lived near Ardath, Saskatchewan.

Our social life revolved around our country church with picnics, quilt raffles, box socials, and choir practice for the adults. Every month or so there was a "Ladies Aid" meeting, an opportunity for mothers and wives who seldom gave themselves a day off to have a chance to talk to someone besides their husbands and children. The men attended, too, visiting outside until the meeting was over and lunch was served. Sunday morning church was a more formal occasion. The services were in Norwegian; the men sat on the right side of the church and the women on the left. There was always a little competition over who should have the preacher and family home for dinner afterward.

During the thirties, camp meetings and tent evangelists, which had been such a feature of rural America, became more frequent on the prairies. I don't remember any "Elmer Gantrys" but when we, our relatives, and neighbours went to "Buckingham's Grove" to join in worship with the Holiness Movement Church who sponsored the tent meeting, the contrast in style was pretty impressive to us laid-back Scandinavians. Bouncy music, emotional testimony, even some pretty loud sermons—all that exuberance was pretty heady stuff to Lutherans, who were more used to singing "A Mighty Fortress Is Our God" and the Doxology. Of course the best part for us kids was when "church" was over and we feasted on fried chicken, potato salad, and Aunt Clara's Lady Baltimore cake as we sat on blankets under the trees.

But even for Lutherans, religion was not always staid and serious. About that time Bible camps were becoming popular. Prairie people found little oases of green beside lakes and springs and camped out for a week, or maybe just made a day trip, to join friends and neighbours in worship and fun, a respite from toil and anxiety, to forget for a little while the burning wind and barren clouds that promised rain and delivered dust.

Pastor Carl Kopperud of Cadillac, Saskatchewan, has fond memories of the Bible camp near Swift Current, Saskatchewan.

Simmie Bible Camp was another of the good things of those years and served our family and church well. If you travel to Simmie over treeless and dry prairie and then continue west, you will come to a hidden valley with bright bubbling springs and beautiful trees. Here our Swift Current area churches established a Bible camp. It was a place of refreshment for both body and soul. The first years we attended everyone stayed in tents. The only building was a small cookshack. We ate out of doors and the meetings were held in a great big tent. These were evangelistic style meetings, and many of our present pastors and missionaries and active lay people in our congregations were saved or came to assurance of salvation during these camp meetings.

We boys would cut off stems of wild rhubarb (cow parsnips?) and use them for peashooters to shoot green chokecherries at unsuspecting girls in that strange adolescent form of love that teases and torments to get the attention of those altogether desirable creatures we professed to hate. I'm sure the stems were poisonous as our lips would burn and swell up, but I don't remember anyone getting sick. We got into trouble when we accidentally shot the pastor's wife, but we never got sick.

We went swimming down at the river. The particular place depended upon wherever the river had washed out a deep enough hole during spring run-off to leave sufficient water. We had to find two swimming holes, one for the girls and one for the boys, as it would never do to have mixed bathing. Sex education was rather simple in those days as it consisted of a simple four-letter word: "DON'T." Don't look, don't touch, don't even think!

George Anthony has happy memories of the United Church Summer Sunday School Camp at McAlister Lake, southwest of Moose Jaw. The lake was small, about twenty acres, George says, and there weren't many trees. He recorded his memories from 1933 in the local history book, *Rolling Hills Review, 1840–1980.*

Summer camps were very enjoyable during the holidays from school. We were allowed to attend, along with other children, perhaps nearly one hundred. They were school students from the various points where church services were held in the country during the summer. The camp usually lasted a week.

The charge for attendance was $1.50, but instead of our father paying for us he suggested we take two cows to

---

18

Tug-of-war game at Sunday School picnic. *Beth Byggdyn*

supply the camp with milk. Earl Christiansen and I milked the cows morning and night.

The campsite was the McAlister yard, where there was an old house and barn and also the McAlister Lake nearby. Mrs. Tom McCrae and Conrad Walz Jr. were supervisors. Mr. Outerbridge, the student minister, was in attendance to take charge of the ministerial work, and give assistance when necessary.

We lived in tents, the yard looking like an Indian village. There would be about ten children in each group, under the name of an Indian tribe, with a chief. We recall the weather being rainy and cold. We had to dig a ring around the tents to keep the rain from getting under them.

Upon rising in the morning, we had a swim in the lake, then breakfast at a long table outside. We had good food, which was cooked in the barn on the premises. No one would go in the house; they thought it was haunted.

We had a boat on the lake and often went for boat rides. We also enjoyed baseball, volleyball, and other games. A treasure hunt was an attraction, but when the treasure was found it was only an old piece of rubber roofing in a gunnysack.

The tribe scoring the most points for the games was to receive a prize, but we were all surprised to be given chopsticks with which to eat peas.

Camp break-up, the last day of camp, people came with wagons, buckboards, old run-abouts, horseback, and most any mode of travel. A campfire was made. Mr. Outerbridge played the violin and everyone joined in a singsong, after which parents took their children home, ending a very successful camping holiday. (Reprinted with permission of the publishers)

GOOD OLD GOLDEN RULE DAYS

Rural areas on the prairies, other than the villages and hamlets, were known by the name of the school district. Each school district was about twenty square miles, and as the farms were small, there were often a dozen families with children and a few bachelors in each district. Hills too rough or rocky to farm, steep coulees leading into the winding creeks, sloughs, brush, and alkali seeps were useful as pasture but cut down on the number of resident ratepayers in a district. And resident ratepayers were the people who initiated formation of the school district, supplied the students, chose the teachers, paid the taxes, and determined the attitude toward education for their families. The size and the formation of rural school districts came under provincial jurisdiction and were governed by the School Act.

The school became the heart of the community. Church services, community meetings, dances, amateur theatrics, political rallies (and polling centres for the resulting vote), sports days, ball games, just about any gathering that involved more than one family took place in or around the school. Local patriotism centred in the school district. Even though some members of the community didn't always get along with each other, when it came to cheering at ball games or comparing Christmas concerts, the home crowd pulled together like family.

Teachers who served in the rural one-room schools often had little professional training. The prevailing notion was that anyone who had successfully passed through high school was competent to teach the lower grades, so a rural school was often the sphere where a young person found out if he or she enjoyed teaching enough to get further training and qualify for more senior, better-paying positions. It is a real tribute to the hundreds of beginning teachers that many of them did so well, handling discipline and preparing lessons with a minimum of resources as well as inspiring "their children" to value learning. There were collateral benefits to the system, too. Many a young farmer found his partner for life among the succession of young ladies who came to take over the classroom. Students who faced a "new" teacher every year had the benefit of their varied talents: one might make math exciting, one be musical, another a whiz at sports or drama. And the young people who found that they hated teaching, couldn't stand kids, and knew that they would never be happy in a classroom usually quit after a term or two. They were not so burdened with student loans and debts that they had to keep a salary coming in, meanwhile making themselves and their charges miserable.

School memories from the thirties aren't all about walking six miles to school, uphill both ways, in bare feet through snowdrifts as they are sometimes characterized. Wallace Byggdyn, a retired pastor, has some very positive school reminiscences.

One of my fondest school memories involves a Mrs. Susanna Kinney, teacher of Ames School, near Eyebrow, Saskatchewan, when I was a lad. Mrs. K. kept good order and taught us well. She also knew how to give us a good time. One Halloween night she packed twelve of us pupils into her Model T and drove us around the rural community. With us we had a "dummy" figure. We'd knock, plunk down the dummy near the door, then hurry out of sight. When the knock was answered, we'd appear, share a laugh with the homeowners, and be given treats.

I remember the Christmas concert when I played the part of a black man. Probably black shoe polish was used to blacken my face. After the concert a man in the community came to me and said it was the first time he'd seen a black man with white ears!

A school Halloween party is also one of Beth Byggdyn's favourite memories from the depression years. She grew up near Prince Albert, Saskatchewan.

My sister, Ruth, and I must have been about eleven and

The school pony-cart. *Eleanor Kopperud*

twelve (I was the elder) when we were permitted to attend a masquerade Halloween party held in the evening at the school. We had attended the school-day parties on October 31 every year since starting school, but to go to an evening affair, and in costume, too, was really special.

There was no money to buy costumes, so, with Mother's help, we improvised. We decided to go as twin pumpkins. Mother dyed our old voile dresses as well as two pairs of our ribbed cotton stockings and two bleached sugar bags a rich dark green. Two bleached flour sacks she dyed a bright orange. These she made into two pairs of bloomers with elasticized waists and leg openings. The green sugar bags, with slits in them for our eyes, noses, and mouths, were slipped over our heads. The green dresses, being of light material, tucked nicely into the full orange bloomers that we stuffed with wadded paper to make them puff out. The green stockings provided us with "roots" or maybe vines. We had a great time at the party and nobody guessed our identity until we removed the sugar-sack masks.

Costumes are a part of school memories for Dorothy Gessell of Strasbourg, Saskatchewan.

Track and field as part of school activity was enjoyed by all four of us children. Mother made uniforms for us out of sugar bags and trimmed them with our school colours, purple and gold. I won ribbons for various jumps and races. My brother Kenneth's specialties were shot put and racing. John was pretty good in everything, but Donald was the best runner. His last school track meet saw him so far ahead of the others that he turned around and watched them come up to the finish line.

The winners of our local meet went to Weyburn to take part in a larger event. We travelled in a three-ton truck, sitting on benches in the open box, each of us equipped with lunch and a blanket. One year on our way home, it began to rain. The road had very little gravel on it so it was hard to keep the truck on the road. When we reached the hamlet of Forward, the driver, concerned for our safety, turned into the little schoolyard. We trooped in to the school, wet blankets and all. Our teacher got us some crackers and cheese at the store and by pooling that with what was left in our lunch bags we all had our "hunger pangs" taken care of.

Each older pupil took a younger one as partner, and we bedded down on the floor. My little friend kept throwing her leg on top of me, and every time I shifted it, back it came a couple of minutes later. What with whispers, giggles, and snoring, we didn't get much sleep. In spite of still slippery roads, we were delivered home by noon the next day. After dinner I made up for lost sleep until Mother woke me so I wouldn't miss my favourite radio program, *Charlie McCarthy*.

Avis Haug who lived near Ardath, Saskatchewan, especially remembers the road to school.

In the summer, when old enough, we walked to school. I remember my brother Harvey killing gophers—with his lunch kit! Later on all three families of us cousins had Shetland ponies and carts. Bicycles didn't come into it until the forties. There was one family that was always late for

The caboose kept children warm on frosty rides to school. *Eleanor Kopperud*

school, and they were punished by having to stay in at recess. When I was a beginner, Dad took me to school in the truck. But one morning it wouldn't start for quite a while. When it finally did, I knew I would be late and refused to go at all, for fear of having to "stay in."

Rides to school in the caboose went along with winters. Sixty below or not, Dad and the faithful farm horses made the two-and-a-half-mile trip to school twice daily. The little stove with its chimney through the roof of the caboose kept us warm.

A farmer close to the school flooded a large rink for us school kids, and Dad made us a smaller one in front of our house. At that time we had a "newcomer" from Norway, Peter Volden by name, staying with us. Peter could ski, of course, but had never been on skates. We finally persuaded him to try and gleefully anticipated watching him fall. But he didn't, and as we watched from inside the house we were so disappointed we nearly cried.

Joy Mitchell (nee Priestley), now of Mitchellton, and her sister Roxie had to live with their grandmother in Readlyn, Saskatchewan, for a while. Her mother was widowed and did housework to make ends meet but had no other way to provide schooling for her girls. After her mother remarried, the family was reunited, and Joy remembers the trips to school with her new dad.

Dad drove us to school with horses and buggy. We had what was called a Bennett buggy. Later on I became the driver in the summer months. In winter, Dad drove us with sleigh and horses. It was really cold so we had lots of blankets, and also a foot warmer—a large rock that had been heated in the oven overnight. There was lots of snow and many drifts so we had a bumpy ride, which we loved!

School parties were a big event in children's lives, recalls June Mitchell, who lived in the Galilee area of Saskatchewan.

My sister Phyllis remembers how they looked forward to the annual Valentine party. For weeks ahead, they cut out figures from the Eaton's catalogue coloured pages, and with flour and water glue, pasted them on paper hearts. If they were really ambitious they decorated them with a bit of ribbon or lace. All ages, little tots to grandparents, came to the party. It was quite an event, and perhaps, just maybe, one would receive a Valentine from a secret admirer!

Many of the teachers in rural schools during the hard times of the thirties could relate to the experiences of Gwen Lowe (nee McKillop). It was not an easy life, but it could be interesting. She wrote of her 1932 teaching experience in a local history book.

I began teaching in the Don Jean School District of Saskatchewan in February of 1932. Teachers' salaries had dropped over 50% that year. I signed a contract for $450 for ten months teaching. This included working with youngsters from Grade One to Grade Ten. The Grade

Eleven and Twelve scholars used government correspondence courses. I never did get all of my last month's wages.

Room and board at the Rosso home cost me $18 a month. I shared my room with Vera Gracia, who worked for Mrs. Rosso. This room was part/of an addition to the main house, and almost no heat could reach it. About four o'clock on cold winter afternoons Mrs. Rosso put two large stones in the oven of the kitchen stove. At bedtime these stones were wrapped in clean sacks and put between the sheets at the foot of my bed. This helped immensely and was surprisingly cozy.

One of the most pleasant memories I have of the Rosso home is the marvellous Italian cooking: meatballs (I've never tasted better), homemade spaghetti, beef or rabbit that had slowly simmered for hours in wine and spice, homemade cookies for lunch pails. One reason she had such a fine supply of food was that Mr. Rosso had built an ice house, dug into the side of the hill and insulated with a covering of straw. Ice was stored in it in the wintertime. In summer, cream, meat and other perishables were kept there.

Another pleasant memory was the music. Often on Saturday nights the Rosso family and "Curly" (an Italian who worked for them—a very shy man with black curly hair and a generous moustache) and any other friends who happened to drop in all gathered in the large kitchen. With violins and guitars they sang songs they remembered from Italy. Usually they were parts of operas. I have never heard opera music that was more enjoyable. It was sung with a sincere love for the music and for the story behind the music.

Much of the social life of Don Jean and Bay Island schools was closely related because the Don Jean Hall was used for community gatherings, dances, etc. In wintertime the entertainment was usually dances and house parties and in the summer ball games, picnics, and of course, dances. Local musicians supplied the music—usually a violin, guitar or banjo, and piano. The admission was often just 25 cents for men, and the ladies brought lunch. Sometimes there was just a silver collection for the orchestra. After midnight lunch there was usually some entertainment by local people, a Highland schottische or humorous songs using the names of local people. Sometimes I even had the nerve to dance the "Irish Jig." It was inexpensive fun but glorious entertainment.

Most of the travelling was done either with horses or just good old-fashioned walking. I had grown up in the city so I found the horse particularly fascinating in spite of two "run-aways." Cars, of course, were used for longer journeys such as going to town or when a group of us young people went to the opening of the Dunkirk Hall.

By 1932 the depression was really taking effect on the economy. Teachers' salaries had slumped. The price of wheat had dropped drastically. Unemployment was getting worse. A late August hailstorm hit the Don Jean and Bay Island area making tax collection even more difficult. It was agreed that some of the ratepayers could pay part of their taxes by giving me "free" room and board, the value to be deducted from my salary. The first three weeks was at the Elliot home, two weeks at their expense and an extra week was given to pay part of a bachelor's tax. He had given hay to Mr. Elliot to make up for the cost of boarding the teacher. I often wondered just how much hay that was.

My next move was to McCrae's. My outstanding memories are of the atmosphere of that home—gracious, well-bred dignity without being stuffy or stiff—and the sound of the birds on the lake, hundreds and hundreds of ducks, geese, and swans. It seemed that you could hear them all night long. I finished the school year at the Bono home. Mrs. Bono had only been in Canada a few years and was still learning English. We became good friends, each trying to learn a little of the other's language.

The year ended with the Christmas concert, a combined

effort of Bay Island and Don Jean in the Don Jean Hall. There were pageants, skits, recitations, and songs. Money collected from raffles paid for two Christmas presents for every child—one for pleasure and one more practical. It was a wonderful evening but a sad one too, because it meant saying good-bye to all the friends I had made. The next day I went to Crestwynd in a sleigh drawn by a team of horses to catch the train for Moose Jaw. (Courtesy of the Crestwynd Community Club, compilers of *Rolling Hills Review, 1840–1980*.)

Children of the thirties remember their teachers, the parties, and transportation, but some of the best memories are of recess and noon-hour fun. Carl Kopperud of Cadillac, Saskatchewan, remembers the games and good-natured shenanigans that took place at lunchtime.

Our ball team was very good. We played before school, at recess, and rushed our lunch to get extra minutes at noon. Everyone played. Our girls were outstanding. They could compete with any boys. We would always win the field day. Rules for the meet said that all teams had to have at least four girls, which was no problem for us, but for the town teams where the girls seldom played it was a disaster. Their girls would throw underhanded and jump out of the way of the ball and worry about their hair or finger-nails while our girls would be swatting home runs and sliding in to bases. My sisters, Carolie and Kay, and Dorothy Haakenson could drive a ball as far as anyone. Paula Haakenson was our catcher, no pads, no mask, but nothing got by her.

Spring and fall when we couldn't play ball, we played prisoner's base, pum-pum-pullaway, poison tag, red light, or hide-and-seek. We played some rather dangerous and different games too. We once had a rip-roaring rodeo complete with a race where we stood on the backs of gal-loping teams of horses like we saw in pictures of the

Romans. The horses and children all enjoyed it, and the teacher, who was safely tucked away out of sight on the other side of the trees and the school, never knew what was happening and so enjoyed her lunch in peace.

We had mud and rock fights, made horses buck in the stalls and tried to stay on them, and roasted our sandwiches in the furnace or on a little campfire built on the basement dirt floor. Guardian angels had little time off in those days.

Sadie Goddard, now of Mossbank, Saskatchewan, writes of the horses that helped get her family to school. Although fun to talk about now, they are not part of her favourite memories!

Horses—beautiful horses—running wild—sorrel coats glistening in the sun—colts at their side—poetry in motion! Ah, but the poet never rode to school in a horse-drawn vehicle.

The horses we drove to school were the bane of my younger years. My mother had a lovely little fast pony, Kitty. We lived three miles from the town school and Mother drove us there each morning and picked us up each afternoon until I was nine. (She also cooked, washed, ironed, baked bread, knit, and made all our clothing.) The summer I was nine our farmhouse was destroyed by fire, and after that we spent summers on the farm and winters in town.

This was when our troubles started. We drove ourselves to school. As more kids became school age, the buggy got more crowded, and Kitty got older and weaker. Finally we used to walk up the hills and ride down. Kitty was soon retired.

Next came Paddy, a short, powerful, nasty horse, with a wicked bite. My sister Norah was a capable horsewoman, but even she couldn't handle him. He would bolt at the slightest excuse. Soon the buggy became a wreck.

Next we rode in the wagon. The wagon box was difficult

Ready for the ride to school. *Eleanor Kopperud*

to climb in and out of, never mind that we also had to drive Pete and Barney. Pete was a great tall workhorse, and Barney just went along for the fun. These two workhorses never had it so good. All day long they ate and slept in Hart's stable. By evening they were ready for a romping trip home. Harnessing them was almost impossible. To get the bits in their mouths Norah had to stand on the manger until they opened their mouths. We hitched them to the wagon and quickly clambered in, then hung on for our lives. We really were not in control. At least once a week they ran away with us, tearing through town and racing for home at top speed.

We left the farm. No more horses. Adios amigos.

We Should Have a "Club"

Communities were united by more than the bonds of proximity. At first perhaps it was a common ethnic heritage and language, the same religion, or the same geographic origin of their immigrant ancestors that integrated the prairie pioneers. By the thirties, however, many factors were working to make neighbourhoods more neighbourly. English had replaced other tongues as a working language. Illness and accident happened quickly—and prairie people helped each other when they did occur. Those whose church was not accessible worshipped at one that was. Youngsters attended the same school, grew up, and married. Soon the Jensons, the LaCroix, the McIntoshes, and the Fischers had mutual grandchildren.

In every community, as in a family, there was some disagreement. Jealousy, envy, rivalry, and bickering are inevitably present in any group of humans. Prairie affects people in many ways, but it doesn't turn them into saints. But the thirties brought common enemies: the depression, the drought, and the dust. No one was immune. No one who lived through it was exactly the same person afterward. The community worked together, endured together, played together, and made the world tolerable together.

One of the bonds of community occurred through various clubs that were organized to keep people active and to buoy their spirits. Mrs. Hamilton of Mazenod, Saskatchewan, tells about a Young People's Club that was formed at Ford school during the thirties.

The Depression (and no class was more depressed than the prairie farmer was) brought forth a Young People's Club, born of desperation. The passing years and the hard times had put an end to the school dances. Even the card parties had faded out, so that when times were hardest and money scarcest, the community had a collection of "teens" and "twenties" with no money and no place to go for entertainment.

A meeting was held in the school and with a few suggestions from a young neighbour, experienced in this line, and the co-operation of the teacher, Tony Maas, we launched a winter program. The trustees allowed the use of the school every second Friday night. Each family gave 25 cents in cash to buy gasoline for the two gas lamps, which was all the actual cash needed. Coffee, sugar, cream, sandwiches, and cake were provided according to the list. Every lunch was a feast! At least we had butter and eggs to bake with.

With the Young People's committee, myself, and the teacher acting the part of "policeman-referee" we produced a routine for each meeting that lasted throughout the five years of the club's life. First, something for the mind: the experiences of those few who had been "outside," the stories of some of the best-known operas, debates, and "stump" speeches, among other items, filled the bill. Second came games, both intelligent and boisterous. Next came lunch and a singsong. Last, we had an hour and a half of dancing.

Don't forget that this was a community project, which meant that every young person was entitled to enjoy it. Since in a community there are always those who consider themselves superior, it was necessary to adhere to a few rules. The success of this young people's affair can be attributed to the fact that these rules were thought out before things started and were not the result of unhappy situations. The young people themselves deserve great credit, too, for submitting to restrictions that were quite unpleasant at times. Perhaps without being conscious of it, they acknowledged to themselves that the satisfaction of the whole group must come first or we would cease to be a community.

Here are a few of the rather galling restrictions that were accepted with good grace: no lingering in the porch, everybody inside the school, everybody join in the games, partners quite often chosen by lot to rescue the unpopular, calling "ladies" choice if the poor dancers had been left sitting too long.

The dance music was supplied by anyone who could play anything, with a chorder at the piano. Harold Williams played a good loud mouth organ. Donald and Norman Martin could do the same. Orville Mytroen had played the violin and the mandolin. With all these willing musicians to take a turn no one needed to miss many dances. No building, I am sure, has ever rocked with more truly hilarious laughter or resounded to the beat of happier dancing feet than our old Ford school. The real "whoops" were reached whenever the caller shouted, "Ladies, join your lily-white hands, gents your black and tan!" That no bones were broken was due to good luck rather than good intentions.

Everything was left shipshape by the 1 am deadline—dishes washed by members in turn, furnace shut off, lamps properly out, and horses hitched and ready for home. There must be a lot of people from those days who wonder if their children have half as good a time as they themselves did. (From *Furrows and Faith*, courtesy of the editor, Phyllis Zado)

As a result of my research into the depression era, Tracy Esquirol of North Battleford, Saskatchewan, kindly allowed me access to the diaries of her uncle and aunt, Mr. and Mrs. Martin Iverson of the Meota district. The diaries date from the late 1920s to the mid 1930s. Mrs. Iverson, formerly Frances Ewart, came to the district to teach at Fitzgerald school and, as often happened, married Martin, a young farmer there.

Running through both stories is mention of the "card parties." People of the district took turns hosting on Wednesday evenings. Attendance varied from eight to thirteen tables, meaning that anywhere from thirty-two to fifty or more district people loved to play "500." It was a proper club with officials. Martin mentions being the recorder, keeping track of the scores.

At the end of each season prizes were awarded—ladies' and men's high and low for the year.

The card parties were so important to community members that the diary writers even mention when they could *not* attend, and give the reason that kept them away.

In the late twenties the young people in our Boule Creek district decided to meet for house parties every two weeks. They called themselves the "Humdingers." The word "humdinger" was slang for something up and coming, entertaining, unusual. It is even in the *Oxford Dictionary*: "noun—a person or thing of striking excellence."

When the club started they would play whist or bridge, engage in party games and stunts, and have lunch to finish the evening at each home in turn. It soon evolved into more ambitious projects. They put on dances in the local school and went on excursions, berry picking in the sand hills, or to Cypress Hills Park for a camp out. And, largely under the influence of ex-teachers who had married into the community, they put on three-act plays.

The play I remember best was *Dotty and Daffy*, a farce with sort of the same premise as the modern film *Parent Trap*. Two teenage pals decided that Dotty's father and Daffy's mother should get together, get married, and make them into sisters. The actors who played the father and mother were in real life a married couple. As love interests they had to kiss and such— and, even in play-acting, decorum was properly observed in those days, especially in public.

In 1932 the whole Humdinger club packed up tents, food, kids, and bathing suits, and everything was piled into the back of Uncle Arvid's big truck for a camp out at Cypress Hills. Tents were pitched under the high evergreens near the little lake. Everybody swam, boated, fished, and explored the "forest" as the notion took them. Ernest Thingvold nearly drowned. Breakfast and dinner were potluck, but the supper was "catered" by two families one night and another two the next, taking turns. It made a nice break for the ladies who weren't on deck that evening—a meal where all they had to do was to eat.

AT GLENVERN HALL

DOTTY
AND
DAFFY

Three Act
Comedy
Farce...

Playing Time 2 1-2 Hours

Presented **Humdingers Club** From S.W.
by the of Cadillac
1926--1936

FRIDAY EVG., MAR. 22

Commencing at 8:30

Cast of Characters :

Mrs. Travers	Mrs. O. Kopperud	Daphne Travers	Virginia Lee
Paxton Belmont	O. Kopperud	Aunt Hester Harley	Edna Thingvold
Jack Belmont	Borger Johnson	Alfred Hopkins	John Clements
Freddie Rand	George Bennett	Molly O. Mulligan	B. Bennett
Jimmie Rand	Julian Kopperud	Hilda Johnson	Hazel Johnson
Dorothy Travers	La Verne Reisinger	Hugh Rand	Carl Thingvold

Directed by F. A. Thingvold and Mrs. C. Kopperud

✕ These people have not visited us before, so everybody come, then they'll come back again. ✕

LUNCH Bring Your Own. We Supply Coffee DANCE Music by the Young Orchestra

Admission: Adults 15c. Children 10c.

Glenvern Hall Committee

I have several vivid memories of that camp out, although I was only six at the time. Mother had crafted bathing suits for my sister and me. They were made from the better pieces left of Dad's discarded woolen underwear, and dyed red. They fit fine—until we got in the lake. The suits got longer and longer when wet, until the crotch hung practically to our knees. And then they took a snapshot of us! Even more memorable—our three-year-old cousin, Frayne, had been deposited in a shallow cove to play safely for a few minutes while his mom was busy. Unknown to the grown-ups, the cove was inhabited by leeches. Frayne started yelling and was hauled out with four or five of the ugly things firmly fastened to him. Leeches aren't easily pulled away from their food; they just get longer and longer and will sometimes break off before they let go. Cigarette smokers came to his rescue by touching the lit end to the blood suckers. The heat made them release their grip. The rest of us kids were fascinated, but not enough to go play in the cove.

The Humdinger Club sort of fizzled out by the end of the thirties, but it is still fondly remembered by all the people who were part of a real community enterprise.

Another club that comes up often when talking about the depression era is the Homemaker's Club. Justine Lips, who grew up in Rush Lake, Saskatchewan, remembers:

There was a Homemaker's Club in Rush Lake made up of women of the town. Their purpose was to make life in our little village—about 150 people when I was there—safer and more fun, and also to provide opportunities for everyone to experience "culture" in some form. They sponsored dances, speakers, community suppers, and concerts. They were the reason we had a new town hall, with a stage, and they saw that it was well used.

I particularly remember the plays. My mother, Mary Dantzer (wife of the local general merchant) and Mrs. Butterworth (wife of the high school teacher) really enjoyed directing plays. They would send to Regina for a selection of plays and read them all, trying to picture

Humdinger camp out at Cypress Hills, Saskatchewan. *Eileen Comstock*

which local "actor" would fit each part. I enjoyed listening in on that discussion. One time they chose a three-act play called "Deacon Dubbs." I don't remember the story, but I have clear memories of the stage scenery. Mother got enough wide brown paper from the grain elevator to cover the stage. (The paper was what the CPR used to seal the doors of the grain cars when they were full and ready to roll.) It was very sturdy paper and just the thing to paint on. Mother sketched out a scene of rolling green hills, blue sky, and large shade trees (nothing like the real landscape we had around Rush Lake). The sky was painted with blue calcimine. The hills were light green calcimine, and fluffy clouds were drawn with white chalk. There were fence posts too, coloured with brown chalk, and a large barn or house on a separate moveable panel also coloured with blackboard chalk. Mother spent hours in the cold hall colouring and painting, and sneezing from chalk dust. There was nothing to "fix" the chalk so the actors dared not lean on the fences or they came off with brown stains. Shadows were grey and blue. The whole thing looked pretty spectacular when the curtain was pulled back. That stage set remained in place for years, providing a backdrop for the dance band as well as the singers and speakers who came to perform.

Practising for the play was half the fun. Most of the actors had no experience and had been coaxed into the parts by the two hard-to-refuse women. Learning lines and remembering them was a major problem. The prompter was a very important member of the cast. Usually the actor did a great job of just being himself, no matter what the part, but the audience loved it. Mistakes were part of the show and sometimes provided more laughs than the script.

The directors used imaginative ways to produce sound effects. There was no electricity in our town so stage lights were gas lamps with reflectors. Lanterns and coal-oil lamps provided back stage lighting. Sound effects were provided by shaking rocks in a tub for thunder and banging on pots or pans. Once a telephone was required to ring and the stage manager turned on an alarm clock—a realistic substitute for phone bells in those days. However, the alarm refused to be turned off and rang and rang. The puzzled actor held the receiver to his ear and shouted "Hello! Hello!" into the mouthpiece, but the alarm kept on ringing. Backstage there was hilarious panic, everyone trying to get the alarm stopped. Finally the ample mother of a large family grabbed the offending clock and sat on it, effectively smothering the sound until the spring wound down. The sudden quiet left the actors completely at sea. They looked helplessly at the prompter for a clue. The prompter, who was near hysterics, couldn't say a word so everything came to a halt. The audience wondered what all the gasps and snorts coming from the wings could mean to the plot. As far as the cast was concerned that episode was the highlight of the play. They laughed about it for years.

Another play we kids would never forget was about a time machine. We watched, fascinated, as our mothers entered the magic box and came out as teenagers. The concept was too strange to be real. How could our mothers ever have been that young?

Some of us girls had a chance to strut our stuff on stage as well. The primary school teacher, Sally Peden, learned to tap dance and gave lessons to me and Betty Leach, Audrey Jenkins, and Gladys Meyer. We learned the Waltz Clog, the Sailor's Hornpipe, and other dances and became quite in demand when concerts in our town and surrounding villages needed another act. Our mothers made costumes, white blouses, black velvet shorts, white crepe paper neck and wrist ruffles, and tall silk hats—cardboard painted with stovepipe varnish. We felt just like the dancers in the "Gold Digger" movies. Stage fright always struck just before we went on stage and we never got through a performance without someone making a mistake, but we always wanted to do it again.

Our town hall was used by travelling professional entertainers, too. There were travel talks with magic lantern slides, chautaqua shows with acrobats and magicians, and poets, writers, and elocutionists who were sponsored by the Homemaker's Club. And of course—politicians. Life would have been so uneventful without that hall and the energetic women who kept it busy. Our little town was really blessed by the Homemakers.

TAKE ME OUT TO THE BALL GAME!

S ports day, field day, track and field, fair—the name varied. Large and small towns usually started their annual sports day with a parade. Organizations and businesses arranged floats. Perhaps a flatbed wagon bedecked with crepe paper flowers and streamers would carry seniors in old-fashioned clothing sitting on rockers; on another wagon big-skirted, western-shirted enthusiasts would be square dancing to music from a gramophone. The local farm machinery dealer proudly displayed the latest in tractors, steel lugs removed in deference to freshly levelled streets. Car dealers provided newly waxed examples of their wares—sometimes even a roadster carrying a pretty girl, waving and smiling grimly as she perched precariously high on the back of the rear seat, or even more scary—balanced on the hood. The local band tried to keep in orderly array as its members played and marched at the same time. Children, with gaudy crepe paper ribbons threaded through the spokes of their bikes, wobbled as they had now to ride more slowly than they ever had ridden on their own.

Last, of course, because nobody wanted to walk behind them, dodging the inevitable steaming deposits, were the local horse men and women, and youngsters on ponies. The horses' coats were curried, manes braided, and tails combed to perfection, and the riders were dolled up too. Wyatt Earp or Annie Oakley would have envied them. They proved there was still a trace of the Wild West in the prairie air.

People in the surrounding districts often added their creativity to the local parade.

Floats depicting the Fathers of Confederation or the Natural Resources of Canada were some of many floats in the thirties. One of these, put together by Creemore

School in the middle of the depression, bore a banner: "Join Us and Beat the Depression." On a dray was a fanning-mill with several children busily operating it. They put dogs into the mill. (The dogs dropped unseen into a box below.) At the other end of the mill, out rolled wieners, which were hastily seized by another group of children, dressed as chefs. The wieners were slapped into buns and sold to the bystanders at a nickel each. They were doing a thriving business! To add reality and humour to the scene some of the younger children kept running out among the crowd, picking up the odd (handpicked) little dog, and handing it up to those operating the mill. This float won much applause and laughter. As long as people can laugh at and with themselves, nothing, not even a depression, can beat them. (From *We, of Excel*, with permission of the publishers)

If it were an agricultural fair, there were usually rows of long tables, set up in the curling rink, where garden vegetables, miniature sheaves, samples of grain—wheat, oats, and barley—embroidery, knitting, pickles, jelly, and of course quilts were displayed, studied, and admired. Schools provided samples of children's art and penmanship. Men went through the exhibits quickly, but the women took their time, privately criticizing the judges' placement of ribbons and vowing to put in their own entries, next year.

There were usually races and peanut scrambles for the little kids before the ball games started. The ball games were considered by most to be the *raison d'être* of the whole day. Occasionally, if the purse was generous, barnstorming teams from afar entered the competition, sometimes black teams from the United States. Blacks at that time were not allowed to play professionally in the States. When they came here they provided an exotic challenge to western prairie people, who seldom saw a black man. They were good, and usually took the purse, although once in a while a local team beat them, becoming celebrities in their own right—at least until the next ball tournament.

Most towns put on a Dominion Day sports day on July 1st. All the country round gathered to watch the parade and take part in the fun. Harvey Haug lived near Outlook, Saskatchewan, and remembers:

One of the things that we as kids really looked forward to was July 1st in Outlook. Mind you we had our chores of work that had to be done before we could go. As dry as it was, the weeds and potato bugs seemed to thrive quite well. The garden had to be clean of weeds and the bugs picked off the potato plants if we expected to go.

The big day finally came, and were we excited! You bet we were. We always went together with my aunt and uncle who lived nearby. We would get in the old '28 Chevy truck and head for town. Mom and Aunt Agnes would pack food and made our headquarters at my great uncle's place not far from the fair grounds. I can't really understand why we didn't take the ferry to cross the river. Instead we drove to Betalock, west of Outlook on the other side of the river, and walked across on the railway bridge. I remember (or maybe I was told so often that I think I remember) that once it was quite windy and my cap blew off, landing in the river below. Oh well—who cared! We were headed for July 1st.

I am not sure, but we likely got no more than $1 to spend between us, which seemed a lot in those days. The main entertainment was baseball. Most of the towns around would get a team together and bring them in. Of course there was bingo, wheel of fortune, and other games of chance. Our money went on candy, pop, and ice cream. We had a hey-day and went home tired and happy.

Playing ball on July 1st was the highlight of the summer for the Hagen family who lived on a farm near the village of Hagen, Saskatchewan. According to Helen Salte, now of Outlook:

The love of ball playing was evident to anyone who might

drop in at our yard on the farm, particularly on a Sunday afternoon. The front lawn became the ball diamond. And in back of the house everyone practised pitching, catching, and batting regardless of the risk to the house windows. This was in addition to the weekly team practices. My dad, Hans, was the team pitcher, his brother the catcher, and with cousins and sons, there were five Hagens on the Hagen men's ball team. Of course we girls had our own team, as well. Though our games were not considered quite as exciting as the men's were, we were quite serious about them, and also made up a good part of the cheering section for the rest. On July 1st the team headed for St. Louis for its annual sports day. The rest of us piled into our car to join the crowd. On that day distance didn't seem to be an issue. Some enthusiasts even made the trek in horse-pulled wagons. The crack of the bat, the plop of a ball in a glove, fielders picking off fly balls and grounders, the cheering of the crowd—excitement was in the very air.

Of course to keep up one's strength it was necessary to have a good supply of food and water. What better café than the car, with plenty of sandwiches and goodies. As well there was the bonus of delicious ice cream cones at the concession stand.

All good things come to an end, and we had to head home before dark to get chores done, the house straightened, and ourselves washed up. Our beds were a welcome sight. Next morning we may have moved a bit slower, indulging a few sore muscles. Two topics dominated the conversation—a review of the previous day's games, play by play, and even more important, the question, "When is the next sports day?"

Way down on the scale of grandeur came the local school picnic, although it was sometimes called a "sports day," too. Sometimes it was a trip to a nearby holiday spot, as was the case at Fitzgerald school in 1931. Frances Ewart, the teacher, records:

The Hagen, Saskatchewan, ball team. *Helen Salte*

An ideal day for a picnic. Most of the kids managed to be present. It was dreadfully hot, and how they did enjoy the water. I had fourteen in my car. Ten inside and four outside on the running board. The picnic was at the Turtle Creek. (From the diary of Frances Iverson, nee Ewart, who taught near Meota, Saskatchewan, with permission from her niece, Tracy Esquirol)

Furrows and Faith, the local history book of the Rural Municipalities of Sutton and Lake Johnstone, Saskatchewan, sums up the school sports day this way:

School sports days were usually an early May happening in the early years. Various schools competed against each other, cheered on by their local supporters. Picnic lunches were packed for dinner, and the whole family attended if at all possible. The day traditionally ended with ball games with friendly rivalry between the teams. (With permission of the editor, Phyllis Zado)

At our local school, Boule Creek, southwest of Cadillac, Saskatchewan, the last day of school was usually devoted to a sports day. The board members spent the morning measuring and marking twenty-five, fifty, and one-hundred yard spaces for foot races on the smoothest part of the school yard. They filled gopher holes on the ball diamond and measured out base lines for hardball and softball. They spaced nails an inch apart on two-by-fours to hold the bamboo cane binder whip that we were to jump over, dug the posts into the ground, and spaded up a rectangle of the hard dry sod to make the jumpers' landing a bit safer and softer. They took the platforms (which had been used as a stage for the Christmas concert) down from the barn rafters and put them against the east wall of the school, behind home plate, to protect the siding boards.

Meanwhile the Boule Creek men's hardball team members erected a booth on another side of the school. It was furnished with tubs of ice water to cool the pop, and rickety shelves to hold boxes of chocolate bars, popcorn, and penny candy. The whole edifice was sheltered from the sun with binder canvas tacked onto makeshift rafters.

Families started gathering about one o'clock. There were races for everyone—straight sprints, potato sack races, three-legged races, egg-in-spoon races, and of course the pre-school races, where everybody, from the toddlers barely able to walk to the sturdy five year olds, all ran together and everybody won. Mothers raced; even some of the fathers competed. There were long jumps, hop, step and jumps, and high jumps over the binder whip. There were ribbons—red for first, blue and white for the runners-up.

Then school softball teams played their game. A neighbouring school, perhaps Andersonville or Beaver Valley, was usually invited to compete. We had practised at recesses and noon hours for weeks. We were in top form: girls as well as boys could throw to first from left field, smash a line drive between shortstop and second, or snatch a fly ball on the run. We were in deadly earnest, and the only snag was that the board had bought a brand new softball for the occasion. White and solid, it stung our ungloved hands. We were accustomed to the soggy grey ball we practised with—the one that had its seams renewed with black waxed thread every other day or so. The new ball went far and fast though when we connected with the bat. The audience was great. They cheered for everybody.

Afterwards, mothers brought out sandwiches and cookies, gathered their offspring, got the worst of the grime off faces and hands, and urged the pop and candy sated children to eat something healthy.

Then the hardball game started, Beaver Valley versus Boule Creek. Young farmers, with few gloves but with quarter-inch callouses on their palms, ranged in age from those just finished public school to the grey haired and the bald. Hardball might have been the climax of the day for adults, but we kids didn't much appreciate it. Too slow and boring. The pitcher kept checking runners on first and third and took forever to actually throw the ball. The umpire kept yelling "strike" when it was quite clear to us that the batter hadn't even moved. Batters came to the plate, stood there a while, and went back to the bench. About the only excitement was an occasional "hot-box" when everyone started yelling "go back" and "keep going" all at the same time. Most of the time the outfielders just stood there with nothing to do. Even the booth was closed.

We welcomed the lengthening shadows that meant the day was nearly over, not that we would ever admit that to a grown-up.

A Song in Our Hearts

It is almost impossible to imagine a young person now without tapes, CDs, a boombox, or a radio tuned to continual music. Music was homegrown in the thirties, and surprisingly universal. Few homes were without a musical instrument or two, maybe a violin or guitar, an accordion, various horns, and often an organ or piano—souvenirs of a time when money was a good deal more plentiful. Some people had come to the prairies with musical training and passed it on, but many just picked up the skill on their own. Playing "by ear" was not considered at all exceptional.

Family orchestras were common. My dad and his brothers and cousins played for many dances in schoolhouses, barn lofts, and local halls. Everyone came, young and old. Admission was "25 cents for men and ladies bring lunch."

Jean Freeman, now of Regina, Saskatchewan, started attending barn dances at the ripe old age of three.

I remember, as a three or four year old (1937 or 1938) being taken to barn dances at a big old barn outside our small town (Weyburn). The dances were held in the hayloft, and there were wooden benches all around the perimeter of the loft where people could sit to rest. The coats were usually thrown in a pile in one corner, and the babies and small children were bedded down there. The older kids ran around, played hide-and-seek, and drank orange Crush or still grape. (I guess there must have been Coke in those days, but I don't remember it.) At midnight the local ladies would have huge plates of sandwiches. I remember canned salmon on fresh homemade bread and granite pitchers of fresh boiled coffee from a wash boiler on the wood stove in the kitchen on sale at a makeshift counter—a couple of boards laid across two sawhorses.

The band was always a local group, usually a piano, bass (perhaps a boom bass made from a broom handle and washtub), drums and fiddle, and/or an accordion. Sometimes there were novelty instruments like the washboard or spoons, and once in a great while someone might sing, but mostly it was dance music, period. Waltzes, military schottisches, quadrilles, polkas, and two-steps. And if there were a caller handy, there would be square dancing. I imagine the men slipped away to their cars and trucks from time to time for a smoke and a nip or two, but I don't ever remember anyone being drunk or getting into fights. Barn dances were family events, and the place where most of us learned to dance and to socialize, getting up to waltz or do a schottische with mothers or cousins. And when the evening was over the sleepy kids would be scooped up from the pile of coats and packed into the back of the family sedan for the trip home. I have no idea what it cost to attend a barn dance, but I know it couldn't have been much—maybe a quarter? Maybe less? But it was an inexpensive, fun way to spend an evening.

Justine Lips grew up in Rush Lake, Saskatchewan, and fondly remembers the local dances.

From quite an early age I used to get excited about dances. In our town when we held a dance whole families came from miles around. Everyone brought something to contribute to the lunch—sandwiches or cake—and the sponsors of the event supplied coffee. If there was any other entrance fee I do not remember being aware of it, but I guess they paid the band somehow, and heat for the hall must have cost something. What concerned us girls was what we were going to wear, and who would ask us to dance. There were children of all ages there—babies sleeping on tables in the corner and toddlers sound asleep on mother's shoulder, as well as children interested enough to try to dance. I guess we started dancing with the dads and then with each other—the girls, that is. I think the boys must have learned at home, or waited until they felt like risking asking a girl. I know it took a long time before I danced with a boy my own age. The dads were good sports, though, and dutifully escorted each other's daughters around the dance floor enough so that we wouldn't be wallflowers all the time. Gradually we got to know young people from other districts, and what a thrill when a boy you hardly knew came over and claimed you as a partner. The best fun was dancing the squares. Everyone could be guided through those even if they weren't familiar with the steps, and swinging your partner seemed to be a male competition to see if a girl could be swung off her feet.

There was some unwritten rule that all the boys should congregate on one side of the hall and all the girls on the opposite side. When some brave soul decided he wanted to ask a girl to dance he would have to march across the empty space in the centre—with everyone watching—and hope she would say "yes" or he would feel like a fool. We girls would watch him come, trying not to make eye contact because we couldn't really tell who he was headed for. Emily Post would have frowned at the etiquette. Sometimes the boy would stand in front of you and say "Dance?" and go on to the girl beside you if you shook your head. Others would put out their hand and haul you to your feet without asking at all. Some of them told me years later that they used to confer with each other about who would ask whom for each dance—pumping up their confidence, I suppose. I guess we girls did that too; I know there was a lot of agonizing over the "ladies choice" numbers!

When I turned sixteen, my Detroit aunt sent me a dress that must have been hers for some special occasion. It was more beautiful than anything I had ever seen before—a pale aqua chiffon with a Bertha collar that came over the sleeveless shoulders, a dropped waist, and multi-layered skirt with an irregular hem. It was longer than I usually wore my dresses, and the skirts and collar floated gently in the breeze I made as I moved. It made me feel like a princess. But where on earth could I wear that, in my social circle? Why, to the next dance, of course.

It took a lot of courage to remove my coat that evening. I felt so overdressed. But my friends all told me they liked it, and after my father waltzed me around the floor in his "duty" dance I relaxed and began to enjoy the way the skirt swirled around my knees as I moved to the music. I was asked to dance quite a lot that evening, and then the most surprising thing happened. The band began to play a currently popular song called "Alice Blue Gown," and suddenly I felt as if everyone but me knew a secret because I kept getting knowing smiles and nods. I still don't know if the band played it just for me, but I was as thrilled as if they had. The words seemed made for my dress.

> I was both proud and shy as I caught every eye,
> And in every shop window, I primped passing by.
> Till it wilted I wore it,
> I'll always adore it—my sweet little Alice-blue gown.

June Mitchell recalls that dances were often held in the local school in the Galilee district of Saskatchewan.

Everyone enjoyed the schoolhouse dances. Once in a while the dance would evolve into a box social or pie social in which each woman took a pie or box of lunch to be auctioned off. The auctioneer usually started bids at 25 cents and most pies sold for 50 or 75 cents. The buyer then ate lunch and the pie with the lady who brought it. I remember once when the young men decided to bid up one of their pals, who was socially obligated to buy his girlfriend's pie. The poor fellow had to pay $2 for the pie, which was practically sweepstake money. The girl, who didn't know about the plot, was elated, of course. She also didn't know that it took every penny he had to pay for it.

We sometimes walked three or four miles to a dance and had to stay until it was light enough to walk home. In the early thirties the music was mostly mouth organs. In later years self-taught musicians played the fiddle, ukulele, banjo, and guitar. They learned tunes from records, and by the late thirties from the radio.

Many districts had bands, usually led by a volunteer bandmaster. Any man who could play a band instrument was recruited. The bands would perform at sports days, agricultural fairs, and local celebrations. I remember standing on the balconied roof of Grandpa Kopperud's veranda watching and listening to the Cadillac band practise while they marched up and down the road nearby. I was so proud of my dad because he had the biggest horn—a tuba. The Cadillac band was sort of an "on again, off again" group, led by Fred Wertzler, the town barber, who was also the mainstay of a local orchestra.

Viceroy, a little community in south-central Saskatchewan, was fortunate enough to have local leadership when its band was organized. The community history book, *We of Excel*, contains a description of the band, which started up during the depression.

Viceroy has been fortunate in having talented bandmasters. The Viceroy Jubilee Band was formed around 1935 under the able leadership of W. R. Seibert. This band won a provincial championship in its class. It also provided musical education for many children of the district who would otherwise never have had this opportunity. Following the death of Mr. Seibert, the band continued under the leadership of Oliver Mossing. The band continued to be successful and took several prizes in band contests and events. (With permission of the publishers)

The school "rhythm band." *Avis Haug*

Music teachers were available in Saskatchewan, even during the thirties. In our district we were lucky to have several. Mrs. King, a widow in Cadillac with two boys to raise, taught piano in her little house. A lady from Shaunavon travelled by train to teach violin. And the druggist's daughter from Admiral also came by train, giving lessons to a local family in return for the use of its piano when teaching her other students. These teachers charged 35 cents for a half-hour lesson, a bargain indeed.

When I was about seven, Dad bought Aunt Hannah's pump organ for $25 and brought it home in a bobsleigh so that we girls could learn to play. We went to Cadillac for lessons when the folks could afford it. It was hard to scrape up the money, but Mother—who loved music although she couldn't sing or play herself—insisted that because we had inherited Dad's talent we had to learn. We didn't like to practise and didn't much appreciate our folks' sacrifice at the time. I remember one hot summer day, when my sister Carolie, about seven, and I, a couple of years older, had to walk the seven miles to Cadillac, carrying our music satchels. Dad was too busy to take us, although he would come and pick us up at suppertime. We were sent off with warnings not to accept rides from strangers. Mom needn't have worried. No one else was on the road. After about four miles we started gazing back down the road through sweaty eyelids—hoping to see a car, a wagon, or any vehicle. We would have probably accepted a ride from the devil himself, but he didn't appear either.

We learned to play, and so did the three younger kids. One of my best memories is of cold winter evenings when we coaxed Dad to tune up his violin. Carolie and I accompanied him on the organ and guitar, chording to the lilts of "Life in the Finland Woods" and "The Devil's Dream" while Mother sat listening, beaming with pride.

IMAGINATION AND INGENUITY

It is hard for today's kids to imagine being happy without their electronic toys. Imagine—no television, not much radio, no computer games, movies maybe once or twice a year—weren't we bored to death?

Those were different times back in the thirties, different families too. For one thing, there were very few "only" children. Most of us had homegrown playmates, brothers and sisters. All of us had some chores we were responsible for—perhaps feeding and watering chickens, washing dishes, or maybe dusting—the jobs varied, but one thing remained constant. Work had to be finished before we were free to play.

I cannot say we were never bored. It was just that, in most homes, as in ours, it was not something to be said lightly to a grown-up. We seldom said it to my mother, who had an overflowing well of great ideas to keep bored kids occupied. Ideas like cleaning out the knives-and-forks drawer, polishing shoes for Sunday, tidying the closet, or filling up the woodbox. These wonderful ideas were nothing you could approach with a "take it or leave it" attitude either. Once Mom told you to do something, you might as well get at it. It is surprising how inventive our young minds could get after finishing whatever diversion Mom had suggested.

Dorothy Gessell of Strasbourg, Saskatchewan, remembers how imagination and ingenuity made for a happy childhood.

Father had a special chair called a "Morris Chair" that could be made into a single bed if needed. Each chair arm had a lion head carved at the front. Don and I would each sit on an arm with twine through the open mouth of the lions. We would have "pretend" horse races, or round up the cattle of the "ranches." Sometimes we sat together on the seat, while our team of horses took us wherever we wished to go.

The tiepost where farmers tied their horses after driving to town was near our home. We enjoyed watching them and wished we had horses of our own. We made harness from straps, belts and twine, and each of us took turns wearing it while pulling the other one around in our little red wagon. We played road hockey in winter with rubber sealer rings holding magazines on our legs for shin pads, and a good supply of "road apples" available at the tiepost for pucks. Skis were fashioned from old barrel staves with strips cut from inner tubes nailed across to keep them on our feet. We dug tunnels in snowdrifts that piled high against the snow fence along the railroad track.

One year Donald's best friend got a Monopoly game for Christmas. Don borrowed it and drew a copy on cardboard. He carved numbers on potatoes and used them to stamp out monopoly money in various amounts. With buttons for players we spent many happy hours exchanging money and real estate. Mother glued a calendar picture of dogs playing poker onto some thin wood. This was cut into small pieces with a fret saw. When we got tired of doing the resulting jig-saw one way, we turned the picture-side under and did it upside down. Don made stilts for us from some discarded lumber, and we soon mastered the art of walking with them. Once he found discarded coil bedsprings that we tied to our shoes and tried bouncing on them. Brand new toys were scarce, but we were resourceful. Toy tractors were assembled using empty thread spools, elastic bands, and the stick from a wooden match. We built large houses on the floor using discarded playing cards as dividers. Eaton's catalogue provided me with paper dolls.

In the attic Mother stored an old suitcase full of costumes she had sewn over the years. At Halloween and ice carnivals this was a real treasure chest. With various items from the suitcase and some imagination we occasionally even came up with prize-winning costumes.

Our days were filled with so many things to do that we were never bored. Our parents talked of "The Great Depression." Donald and I wondered what that really meant. We never felt under-privileged, life offered so much. It was a great time to be growing up as far as we were concerned!

Marion McGillvary and her brother used their imaginations to enrich their play. In a story about their childhood, Marion (who calls herself Marcia in this version) tells us:

Doug and Marcia had been to the fair in Moose Jaw. In their eyes, this first fair they had ever been to outdid all fairs they would ever afterward see. They had a difficult time getting to sleep because their minds were full of the rides, the side shows, the games of chance, the crowds, the smells and tastes and sounds.

The following day they hauled a tub out into the yard. Doug climbed up onto it, holding a rope. He was the ringmaster. As he spun the rope round and round, imaginary bears and dogs took their positions. He called, "Fair is on," and the bears and dogs did their tricks as he snapped the rope. He called "Back to your homes," and the bears and dogs leapt back to their pedestals. He called another group of animals to do their tricks.

Marcia, who was acting the barker's role, was a few feet away calling, "Come and see the world's most ferocious tiger. See the Great Campanella boss the big tiger. See the seven pure white dogs. See them ride their bicycles."

It didn't always take a circus or fair to inspire the McGillvary youngsters into acting.

It was an election year. *The Western Producer* was full of it. It had even become the most popular topic in *The Young Cooperators*.

Doug and Marcia became interested. Soon it was being expressed in their play.

The tub was turned upside-down again. This time it was the rostrum for the politicians. Marcia was the first speaker. She was R. B. Bennett. She had memorized a poem from the paper and now shouted it out with great gusto.

> Mackenzie King is an awful man.
> He soaks his hooves in a big dishpan.

Then it was Doug's turn. He was Mackenzie King. He too had memorized a poem. His poem was about Mr. Bennett.

> All his promises are rot.
> When he's in, they're all forgot.

Marion sometimes wonders if that is where her brother got his start as a political columnist.

Ingenuity is necessary when something gets into such poor shape that its original purpose is altogether frustrated. Wallace Byggdyn, who grew up near Eyebrow, Saskatchewan, gives a good example:

I was the third eldest child in a family of four boys and a girl. My brothers and I were only a year apart. We had one bicycle, which a neighbour had sold Dad for next to nothing. Soon its chain broke so the pedals were useless except to put our feet on. And with four boys using one bike, we were always fixing tires. To get a good ride, despite these shortcomings, we would fasten the bottom of an old tub onto our back, then with the wind behind us, we would get a fine ride, especially if it were downhill. Another idea we had was to fasten the bike to the back of the hayrack when the rack was being used to haul hay or sheaves. The trick was to keep the bike upright, as the rack didn't travel very fast. Sometimes we did manage to do that. It required a good sense of balance!

Lawrence Dornan (left) of Cherill, Alberta, and his brothers and sisters did not lack imagination. *Lawrence Dornan*

Many pleasant memories centred on the games played at the kitchen table, games like crokinole, pick-up-sticks, jig-saw puzzles, and of course card games. Some people (including my grandmother) thought a regular deck of cards got a little too close to being the devil's playthings, so the only decks we played with were ones especially designed for Old Maid, Authors, or Flinch. Flinch cards really resembled ordinary ones, except that instead of having pictures of kings, queens, and jacks, they were numbered. Apparently the devil doesn't have as much affinity to numbers as he does to pictures.

After the Christmas break, our rural school, like many others, didn't open again until the middle of February. My sister Carolie and I spent a lot of the holidays playing "Paper People" at the kitchen table.

Paper People houses were cardboard boxes. With the flaps cut off, a good-sized box could be laid on its side, thus making a two-storey house. The inside of the box was divided into kitchen and living room, and with a serrated bread knife, we cut out bits of the walls to make windows and doors. The top surface was supposed to be the floor of the bedrooms and bathroom. These rooms didn't have windows, or for that matter walls, except in our imagination. We did cut out a place for the stairwell, but long experience had taught us that it was impossible to make steps that would stay in place or even look like a staircase, so the stairs were imaginary, too. Furniture was created from cereal-box cardboard, easy to cut and bend. The bathtub was the inside part of an Eddy's match box, while the outside sleeve had chunks cut out of the top and bent up to make seats—that was the car.

A sample book that came from Uncle Herb's store furnished wallpaper, and if it took several patterns to do up the living room that was all right. We made flour and water paste to stick little pieces of coloured cloth (culled from the ragbag) to the top of the window holes for curtains. Heavier pieces of material gave us carpets for the living room and bedrooms—an amenity that we didn't have in our real home.

Our families were cut from an old catalogue, due care being taken to make sure that the inconsiderate catalogue makers hadn't covered important parts like arms and legs with printing and prices. My sister was more maternal than I. My family was mother, father, one boy, and one girl. Carolie's consisted of mother, father, about six assorted children, and three or four babies. To facilitate seating them in cars and chairs they were always folded appropriately at the hips and knees. Of course, that meant that when they were put to bed, their legs waved around in the air, but that was a minor detail.

Carolie and I were the giants. I spent a lot of time trying to create better furniture, and Carolie spent most of her time interacting with her paper family. (Today, I am the one who tries to write, paint, and work with clay; Carolie is a people person, everyone's friend.) Mother was very patient about the mess we made with paper, cardboard, paste, scissors, and boxes. She called it "clean dirt." We did have to dismantle our creations at meal time, but went right back at it again afterwards.

Nowadays it is possible to buy toy houses fully furnished, with family included. In fact, I bought one at a garage sale when the grandkids were little. They pretty well ignored it. There just isn't much play value in things where someone else has done all the creative stuff. The grandkids much preferred old cardboard boxes, a pair of scissors, and a catalogue. Even that seems a long time ago now. I must add that every time we eat breakfast in a restaurant, one of my regrets is that back in my childhood years there were no such things as individual servings of jam in those little plastic tubs. The tubs would have made the neatest dishpans and sinks for Paper People.

Another activity dear to the heart of many depression-era children was reading. In my community, the Boule Creek library was housed in the school on five small shelves in a little room leading to the cellar stairs. I spent a lot of recesses and noon hours in that room, avoiding persecution from the schoolyard bullies, as I had no older siblings to protect me. Actually, I probably gained in the process as it was a pretty good assortment of books. *Last Days of Pompeii*, *Tom Brown's School Days*, *The How and Why Books*, *Swiss Family Robinson*—I read and reread them all. In class, we were fortunate to have as prescribed texts the creamy brown Canadian Readers. These readers paid no homage to theoretical systems of "learning to read painlessly" through repetition and boredom but actually included things like poetry by Whittier, Longfellow, and R. L. Stevenson, and excerpts from books such as Dickens's *Nicholas Nickleby* and Sir Walter Scott's *Ivanhoe*.

The most imposing book in the school sat on a spare desk at the back of the schoolroom. The *Webster's Unabridged Dictionary* was about six inches thick. Its faded brown cover enclosed wafer-thin pages, the first half-dozen badly dog-eared and worn. One day in Geography period, my assigned Grade Four lesson included several sentences about camels in Egypt and "dung" that was spread on fields. I raised my hand and asked our young lady teacher what dung was. There was an immediate pricking up of ears among the older pupils. She handled it well, telling me to look it up in the dictionary. I walked to the back of the room, and when I found the word, I could have sunk through the floor with embarrassment. It was not that dung was an obscure concept. I probably knew a dozen synonyms in three languages that were adequate substitutes. It was that I had said it—out loud—in school hours—to a grown-up! How times have changed.

Large towns and cities had lending libraries, but there were no such luxuries in the countryside. The travelling library filled a great need in some districts. In the local history book *Furrows and Faith*, William Robb wrote about the travelling library that was kept at his home on the farm.

From the mid-twenties to well into the thirties, we were in charge of the Travelling Library. It consisted of a box of books, about sixty of them, sent each year by the provincial government in Regina. The books circulated through the district. It was a wonderful thing to have in a long hard winter when we did not do much visiting.

The books appealed to a wide range of tastes, and the neighbours used to look for their favourite authors when a new box came. Some writers that appeared regularly in the collection were Ernest Thompson Seton, Gene Stratton Porter, Louisa May Alcott, Zane Grey, A. Doyle, H. Rider Haggard, Mrs. Humphrey Ward, Hall Caine, and I think Kathleen Norris. I remember offering the farm to anyone who could solve the mystery in *Trent's Last Case*. (From *Furrows and Faith*, courtesy of the editor, Phyllis Zado)

Yvonne Reimer, who grew up in Winnipeg, Manitoba, remembers how much the lending library added to her family's enjoyment.

While we were growing up, Mom insisted we stay in our yard. She didn't care how many friends joined us so long as we stayed put. Except, once a week my brother Ken and I would walk to the library on Williams Avenue, where we were allowed to exchange two books. We were avid readers, and one Christmas I opened the door to find a man holding out a box. He said he was delivering Christmas cheer to the "needy." I immediately said, "But we are not poor!" and then noticed that the box contained some books. I changed tactics and took it eagerly. I don't remember what else was in the box, but I have those books still.

Books came in mighty handy during the six long weeks our house was quarantined because of measles. Measles was a dreaded disease and a big notice was put on the front door "QUARANTINE—MEASLES" for all to see. No one was allowed in or out except my parents as they had had measles when young and were considered immune. I never did get measles, as I was sort of kept away from the rest as they came down with it. Measles no, but chicken pox—yes, and I have the scars to prove it.

Fun in the Sun ... and the Snow

There weren't too many rural mothers who had anything good to say about prairie winters in the 1930s. That was the season when measles, mumps, chickenpox, colds, and flu often kept them isolated for weeks at a time, nursing one sick kid after another as each passed his affliction on to his brothers and sisters. For kids, though, it meant a long winter holiday from school. Rural schools closed for all of January and part of February, making up the required school days at the end of July and all of August. Winter days may have been short and chilly, but my sister and I made the most of them.

Our cousins Alvera and Frayne usually spent a week or two at Grandma Kopperud's—half a mile from our house—just across the pasture. Every day (barring a blizzard), and sometimes even twice a day, we would meet them in the pasture with our sleds and short skis, their toboggan, and their dad's long skis. We climbed the hills, slid down, and climbed them again.

The best part was when we used the long skis as a toboggan. Three of us sat on them at the top of the hill. The middleman's job was to keep the skis beside each other by firmly gripping the foot rigging. The fourth would shove to get us started and quickly flop onto the back end, swinging her legs up for the next one to grab. The start was slow, but with our combined weight the speed increased quickly, and we were carried far into the patch of buckbrush at the bottom. Only once did we come to grief. Alvera was pusher, and when Carolie grabbed her legs she started to yell. The more she hollered the tighter Carolie hung on to her. It turned out that Alvera had just missed sitting on the ski ends and was bouncing along behind, over rocks and hard snow crust, yelling, "Let go!" Her ski pants didn't stand up under the punishment. The hole that was worn reached right in to bare skin, so that meant an early end of play for that day.

Usually we stuck it out until we heard someone calling for us to come home. Though we always had enough energy to climb the hill just one more time, on the way home we were so played out we could hardly make it. Grandpa's big hill gave us hours and days of fun. When we go back to the pasture now, I am always struck by how much it has shrunk. It looks a lot smaller now than it did then.

I don't know how we would have made out on bigger hills. Wallace Byggdyn, who grew up near Eyebrow, Saskatchewan, remembers a really big one from his childhood.

One Christmas afternoon our cousins and we used a bob-sleigh to give us all a ride down a valley hill. One boy stood on the sleigh and steered it by pushing on the tongue. That part was great, but the hard part was getting that heavy sleigh back up the hill again. We had to push it up, and those Qu'Appelle Valley hills aren't small.

Justine Lips remembers the winter in Rush Lake, Saskatchewan, when not only the kids frolicked out of doors.

There were no good sliding hills in Rush Lake. To get anything steep enough to make a toboggan go at a decent speed we had to trudge up the south road about a mile and a half to a field, which, if the snow was just right, provided a pretty good afternoon of fun. Our school was on the highest point in town, but the land rise was hardly enough to coast a bicycle. However, that changed.

A new family came to town, including a teenaged boy who even then showed sign of the talent that would make him a civil engineer some day. Tronson Leach decided to build a hill at the school. He organized the school kids one snowy winter day and instructed us all to collect snow blocks, which the builders began to pile into a structure resembling a large wedge. When finished, the top was twice as high as my small self. It looked huge, and it stretched in a long slope down the descending hill, wide enough to

A toboggan party. *Eileen Comstock*

accommodate a toboggan or a cardboard slider. I am not
sure how they managed to put ice on the surface. They must
have hauled water from the town pump two blocks away.
But when it was finished the slide was slick and fast and had
a series of icy steps leading up to the top, a flat surface for
the toboggan to load up, and a long run that provided
thrills and speed we had never before experienced. We could
hardly wait for recess and often stayed after school to enjoy
the fun. It had to be "flooded" whenever the weather was
cold enough, and we kept it going until the early spring
made it too soft to withstand the traffic.

The most surprising thing to us was that parents
enjoyed it too. The dads helped haul the water for the ice
sometimes, and my dad supplied cardboard boxes from the
store for sliders, which wore out rather quickly. Sometimes in the evening the parents would get together—
leaving us to babysit—and go up to the slide. Then we
would hear shouts and screams and laughter as they hur-
tled down the slide on our toboggans. After, they would
meet somewhere for a bean supper and come home still
full of the excitement and laughter they had experienced
during their energetic evening together. To tell the truth

it was a little embarrassing to us to see the school principal, the town doctor, and mayor of the town acting like teenagers.

We built the slide every year for several winters and influenced other schools nearby to make them as well. It got to be a bit of a competition as to who could build the best one, and it made a wonderful alternative to skating and snowball fights.

The only ice near our home that could be skated on was at Uncle Jul's dugout. It was big enough but always below the level of the land around it. Snow just heaped and piled and stacked on it, often too much to be shovelled off, so we didn't do much skating. But for other kids and young adults, skating and playing hockey were at the heart of winter fun.

June Mitchell who grew up at Galilee, Saskatchewan, recalls how skating was managed near her home.

The hockey games were held on a rink made by flooding a small slough near Fink's Spring, about halfway between Galilee and Mitchellton. The players came from the whole area. Clarence Mitchell, the playing coach, had one of the best teams. His cousins, the Bentley brothers from near Saskatoon, were some of the world's best hockey players. Clarence must have inherited some of the same skills the Bentley boys had.

In our nearby town, Cadillac, as soon as it got cold enough, the young men and boys commandeered the local water wagon and hauled water from the creek to flood the open rink. The board fence around it didn't keep snow off so there was a lot of shovelling to be done all winter long. One can only admire the determination and spirit that kept the rink open during the winter. The guys were hockey crazy and only reluctantly gave up their place at the rink for social skating from seven to nine in the evening, five nights a week.

Every little community had a rink, and most had a hockey

team. Vince Dantzer, who grew up in Rush Lake, Saskatchewan, tells just how avid he and his friends were.

Rush Lake had a good hockey team that used to challenge the teams from surrounding communities. There was no organized competition, just games that could be arranged when conditions were right. The team was usually trans- ported in the back of my father's truck. It was a fairly large truck that had a big box on the back. It was normally used to haul wheat to the elevator or supplies to the store. The whole team could fit into it quite well, and usually a few of the cheering section, too.

One winter day, we piled into the truck and headed for a scheduled game at Herbert, about ten miles away. It was snowing and blowing, but that didn't seem unusual. We planned to get there about 7 PM. The snow came down faster than anticipated, and the wind did its usual number on the drifting snow, piling it in ridges across Highway #1. Soon the drifts were big enough to block the road. We had to stop and shovel our way through them a few times. Then we hit one that the truck could not get through. Everybody shov- elled and pushed, but we were truly stuck and time was flying.

We fellows were used to solving our own problems. We knew there were no snow ploughs likely to come along, but there was a tow rope in the truck. It was attached to the front bumper, and the whole team pulled together. The truck made it through the snowbank, but it took a long time. We finally arrived in Herbert about 9 o'clock and found the rink closed and dark. Nobody was in sight. After all that trouble—no game?

The coach, Mr. Butterworth (the school principal), wasn't going to give up either, so he found out where the Herbert coach lived and knocked on his door. "Where's your team? We came to play hockey!" Well, the team was mostly home in bed, but being good sports, they roused them- selves and showed up at the rink in time to have a game. It was a good game—and of course we won!

Equipment for hockey depended on how flush or broke the team was. They had to have hockey sticks and a puck. Everything else was optional. Eaton's catalogues made good shin protectors, but masks were unheard of then, even among the professionals. Stitches and scars didn't seem to daunt anyone. Dorothy Gessell, who lives in Strasbourg, Saskatchewan, remembers:

All three brothers bore scars from hockey. Kenneth, the oldest, was a goalie. He had no head or face protection, so he had to get stitches on three separate occasions. As far as the rest of his body was concerned, he resorted to a belly protector pad that belonged to the ball team's catcher.

Once brother John got hit by the blade of his opponent's stick. Father took him to the local doctor as there were several slivers that had to be removed, and a couple of stitches to be put in. Suddenly the doctor had two patients. Father fainted as soon as John was fixed. John had to go on a liquid diet until the stitches came out.

The youngest brother, Donald, earned his scar while being goal judge. He took up his official position behind the net and was a little late ducking the puck, so he ended up with three stitches in his forehead.

Dorothy Mazurik, who lives in Winnipeg, Manitoba, also has vivid memories of makeshift hockey equipment.

As kids growing up in the early thirties, we used to play "street hockey." Of course we did not have the equipment hockey players have today. First of all we would wrap an Eaton's catalogue or thick newspaper around our legs to make very sturdy hockey pads. Old brooms would be our sticks, but the pucks were the most interesting and the most guarded. Some were formed of frozen papier mache, others with candle wax, but the pucks I brought were long-wearing, held their shape and were free. Because I was the one who brought the superior pucks, I was allowed to play when the boys played.

You see, I got home earlier from school than the other kids so I was always home when the milkmen and Eaton's home delivery rigs went past—both horse drawn. Well, I would gather what I called "horse pucks" in a shoe box and hide them under the back step. The boys always envied my hoard and one day threatened to spy and find out where I hid them. I took the whole box into Mom's kitchen and stashed them there.

Next morning brought the end of hockey season for me. Mom decided to bake bread. The kitchen got snugly warm. My pucks melted! The smell was nothing like a bakery should smell. Dad walked in and decreed the end of my puck-gathering days, so that meant the end of my hockey-playing career, too.

John J. Molgat grew up in the Ste. Rose Du Lac district, about twenty-five miles east of Dauphin, Manitoba. There were rivers to skate on and bush to temper the wind. However, the community felt that a "real" skating rink was what they needed.

One rite that marked passage from "little kid" to the next stage of pre-adolescence was the skate on the river from the town to the river mouth at the lake and return. To be valid this had to be performed as soon as possible after freeze-up. It was done as a group, the more adventurous taking the lead to find safe passage at rapids where the ice was not of uniform thickness, and accomplishing this adventure held nearly as much meaning for us as the pilgrimage to Mecca does to a Muslim, or at least that's what we thought.

Eventually, Ste. Rose had an open-air skating rink that kept shifting its location: from the schoolyard to an open area behind what is now Lion's Café—to the hollow near Maillard's Creamery, now the Ste. Rose Lumber & Supply—to the hollow just southeast of the railroad bridge, then to the north side of the railway. Before electric service came to town, night illumination was provided by gasoline lanterns on wires strung over the ice surface. Ste. Rose had a hockey team, some of whose star players were young Doctor Gendreau, the Guyot boys—Sarto, Yvioic, and Romain—and the Dames—Lawrence and Buddy.

We small kids would try to emulate them by playing a form of field hockey on the packed snow of the street. Our first sticks were branches carefully selected to have an elbow that gave them the approximate shape of real hockey sticks. Our pucks were two-inch sections sawed off a piece of cordwood of the right diameter, or failing this, a solidly frozen piece of horse dropping of which there was an inexhaustible supply as horses were the only form of winter locomotion, and every store had, in front, beside, or behind it, hitching posts for customers' teams.

Just as the summers of my childhood seem in memory to have been much hotter and longer than at present, so winters seemed to go the other extreme of arctic cold. Sometimes, on still winter nights, walking slowly home from the deserted skating rink under a clear bright sky full of stars, we would stop by telephone poles to listen to the wires humming from the intensity of the cold and we would say that the wires were singing. Do telephone wires still do that, I wonder.

But winter was not the only time of year that provided good fun for kids and adults, alike. Next to Christmas, my sister and I lived for the week in July that Dad took us to camp at Lac Pelletier, a little gem in the hills about thirty miles north of our home. We spent most of our days in the water, so much time that our hair was bleached like straw, our faces dry and peeling, and our feet had dishpan-hand wrinkles. Mom and Dad did the cooking on a metal rack over three stones that surrounded a little camp fire, then tidied up the tent and made up the beds on the ground ready for a kid to take a nap, if one could be found who was dry enough. They spread old blankets on the beach, socialized with other mothers and fathers whose kids were in the water with us, and did a lot of yelling at us about not going out any farther, and wasn't it soon time for us to quit. The acoustics over the water were very poor, so even if we heard our parents, we pretended not to.

Of course, we had to eat, and it was firmly believed, even by us kids, that if we didn't wait for an hour after eating we would be struck by "cramps" as soon as we hit the water and die. So we had time to climb hills, fish for perch, catch frogs, and visit a couple of ladies who had cookies in their cupboard. (Cookies were not considered "eating" for swimming purposes.)

There were few swimming spots in southern Saskatchewan. Oh, there were sloughs and dugouts, but unless it was very early spring, the likelihood of getting the "itch" from little organisms that lived in stagnant water made swimming in them precarious. One dose of the itch was usually sufficient to deter even the most enthusiastic water-baby. That made Lac Pelletier even more precious to us.

It may seem incongruous that we could take a vacation at a lake in the middle of the depression. Let me explain. There was nothing growing that had to be summerfallowed. A neighbour was happy to send his son to feed the hens and milk the cow, and took the eggs and milk as compensation. Dad loaded our Model T with everything that could be needed. Blankets and couch mattresses were stacked on the roof, and an old Winnipeg couch tied upside down on top to keep things from falling off. The back seat was removed, and several large wooden egg crates installed, each filled with potatoes, eggs, bread, jars of milk and cream, sealers of chicken and meatballs, and anything else that could be stored and eaten. Pillows padded the wooden lids and made a pretty good seat for us kids. A coffee pot, frying pan, potato kettle, and a minimum of dishes were tucked wherever any room was available. The old tent, complete with patches where mice had chewed little holes, was tied to one running board, and a little stack of chopped firewood was fastened to the other. At Iverson's beach, on the north end of the lake, it cost $1 a week to pitch a tent under the rows of trees that lined the shore. Dad dug a hole in the shade behind the tent, poured some water in it, and covered it with gunny sacks and a couple of boards. That was where milk and other food were kept cool. Dad usually had to go home to tend to things there after a couple of days, and when he came back he brought more fresh food. I can't imagine that it was much of a rest for the grown-ups, what with sleeping on a dilapidated couch, cooking on the ground, and trying to keep us clean enough to stay healthy and reasonably presentable. I remember Mother bathing baby Kay in a washbasin, crouched on the ground under a twine clothesline where towels were hung to dry. It would be nice to think that we would go to the same lengths for our children, but I am sure glad I have never been put to the test.

My brother Carl has written his memories, and his description of our lakeside holidays is vivid.

One thing that drought and no crops did for us a couple of years was to allow us to go to Pelletier Lake. It was about thirty miles across country, and we packed up the Model T with tent, food, bedding, and even a Winnipeg couch upside-down on top, and made our way along dirt roads and prairie trails to a memorable couple of weeks at the lake. There was an abundance of perch in the lake, and I remember Dad with the bottle-cap scaler, cleaning mess after mess of fish. There were other families there, too, and Carolie and Eileen enjoyed the friendship of many other girls and the attentions of many young fellows. I gained notoriety as being champion tree pee'er. I could shoot higher on the tree than any of the other little boys, and I announced this accomplishment with justifiable pride to the whole gathering of friends and relatives one Sunday. For some reason, Mom did not share my enthusiasm. Carolie loved the water. She went in only once a day, but that was all day. Lake Pelletier was the gathering place for many a family reunion for both the Kopperud and the Lindeblom clans.

Although Justine Lips grew up at Rush Lake, Saskatchewan, that hardly meant there was good swimming during the depression.

There was no water to swim in, in the lake at Rush Lake. The CPR had drained it in 1905 when the railway was built through our area. We never forgave them for it because swimming holes were scarce during the dry thirties. We did have one place that was deep enough to swim in, though. At a place called Fauna, between Rush Lake and Waldeck, the CPR had built a dam on the Swift Current creek and erected a water tower for use of the trains. That dam had a small swimming hole below it and a deeper body of water above it, used by people who could really swim. There were chokecherry bushes growing along the creek and one or two places where one could actually sit in the shade. The bushes also provided changing rooms for those who didn't choose to wriggle out of clothes in the back seat of the car—with towels making blinds in the windows. The highlight of the week in summer was when we filled the car with family and friends and took off the five miles to "the Dam" to swim.

My first swim suit was memorable because of the hat. I think it came from my Detroit aunts, because there was nothing like it in the stores around Rush Lake. It was very stretchy rubber, bright orange with coloured stripes along the edge, and two three-dimensional orange rubber chrysanthemums with green leaves attached to the side. The swim suit was thick wool with a small skirt and really seemed heavy when wet, but I felt like the belle of the ball when I wore it!

I don't think I would ever have learned to swim at the dam. The hole was small (we could not believe how small it was when we went back as grown-ups), and the bottom was squishy and full of weeds and even bloodsuckers. That didn't stop us from getting wet and enjoying the splashing and ducking that went on. Someone always brought a blown-up old inner tube that was great to float on.

There were often families from surrounding neighbourhoods there as well, and sometimes a group of families would plan a picnic together. I often wonder how we managed without insulated picnic coolers and frozen packs in that hot weather. Nobody ever got food poisoning that I heard of. Potato salad and hard-boiled eggs were standard fare. Sometimes we had cheese sandwiches and fried chicken. The drinks were always lemonade, or tea and coffee if the fathers were up to building a campfire. It was necessary to bring wood for the fire because there was very little lying around that could be used. Dad saved wooden packing cases from the store for that purpose. Dessert was pie—usually apple because it carried well, or raisin, which was my favourite. And there were always pickles. I think we must have counted pickles as a "vegetable" on the menu.

In the Weyburn area of Saskatchewan, Jean Freeman remembers that there were several choices for the determined water-baby.

There were a lot of home-grown pleasures too, like going to my great-aunt's farm, where they had a huge wooden horse trough that was filled with water from the dugout by a windmill. It was slippery with moss, and cool and deep enough so it was almost like a small, albeit very narrow, swimming pool. (We had never seen a real swimming pool, except in the movies.) We would put on our crinkle-crepe bathing suits and bathing caps and spend a glorious afternoon splashing in the water—much nicer than the days we went to the creek (very little water and a lot of stones) or the dugout at my cousins' place (too much water, with muddy banks.)

The best of all, of course, was to go to Carlyle Lake, where my parents had honeymooned in a tent, and spend the day on the beach. So much water! We figured it must be almost like the ocean. If you squinted your eyes and pretended, you could sort of blot out the far side of the lake and pretend it was the Pacific! And when it was time to go home, and you were packed, sunburned, sandy, and windblown, into the backseat of the family Ford, you could still feel the waves lapping and lapping on your arms and legs. I haven't felt that feeling in years, but I can still remember it—and it was wonderful.

In Alberta, near Fabyan Station in the Wainwright area, a family named King made use of a swimming hole at the nearby river to help out the family finances. On Sundays, people travelled to King's Park to picnic and swim. There were even sandy beaches to add to the attraction of this oasis in the dry plain. At first, people dressed and undressed in the nearby bush, men having one particular spot by general consent and women, another. Several years later, Ralph King built a bathhouse that could be used for a nickel, and diving boards. It became popular and the old swimming hole was usually full every weekend.

The Kings also put together a sort of booth to serve refreshments, and as they had put up ice in the winter, they made two five-gallon freezers full of ice cream every weekend. Every Sunday morning the family would be busy turning freezer handles to stock their booth at the river.

John J. Molgat's childhood memories of summer at Ste. Rose Du Lac include a lot of swimming as well as other diversions made available by the geography of the Interlake District of Manitoba.

Many of the long, torrid afternoons of summer were spent at the swimming hole of the river in Park Dollard, where by unspoken agreement the boys had a small clearing in the bush as their change room and the girls had similar facilities at the opposite side of the bush. It would have been considered an abominable breach of etiquette to try to sneak into the other's domain for a peek as that would have made sharing of the swimming hole impossible. Sometimes, those of us who had bicycles would pedal along the wagon trails that wound between the hay stacks in the immense flat hay meadows to the northwest of town, all the way to Welcome Beach on Lake Dauphin, bringing with us the essentials for a wiener roast.

My earliest memory of bathing suits is of the cotton jersey variety then most common. You would probably be arrested for indecent exposure if you tried wearing one on a beach today. This material, once wet, would mould itself

(Left to right) Alvera, Carolie, and Eileen wearing the bathing suits made from old underwear. *Eileen Comstock*

to every minute contour of the body like a second skin, revealing, even emphasising, every intimate detail one would normally want to conceal. I was a child then and impervious to any form of sexual stimuli, but I cannot help but wonder now, how teenagers of the time coped with this phenomenon in a society that was incomparably more prudish and up-tight than today's. The male example of this garment even had a little skirt in a futile attempt to salvage a modicum of modesty. Before I was old enough to become self-conscious about this erotic apparel it disappeared with the advent of woollen knitted bathing suits.

Some of the fondest memories I have of that time long past I owe to the kindness of the parents of one of my closest boyhood friends, Dick Furneaux. The Furneaux parents would rent a cabin at Clear Lake during the summer at a time when this resort was just starting its development. On successive summers they invited me for a stay of one or two weeks, and no boy could have dreamed himself a better time. The cabins had been recently built of spruce logs and slabs and were located in a stand of tall conifers so that the air was always saturated with the fresh, outdoorsy smell of pine. Even today the smell of pine brings back memories of those glorious days of summer when all day long we played along the length of the sandy beach.

The late twenties and the thirties in Ste. Rose have been rightly described by many as "The Hard Times." No doubt they were, especially for our parents who had to provide shelter, clothing, and sustenance, and yet I have no feeling of having been deprived in any way. Those years before the gates of childhood shut behind me forever are so full of sunny and joyous memories that like Kenneth Grahame in the prologue to his book *The Golden Age*, I can say—"I certainly did once inhabit Arcadia."

Fashion—Dirty Thirties Style

Recycling is in vogue today, but it's hardly a new practice. Our grandparents recycled—witness the pieced quilts, some made of little scraps of new material not big enough to make into clothing, and others made of the more unworn bits of clothing too dilapidated to be used in its original shape. Quilts that survived their original purpose of keeping the family warm in frosty bedrooms can now be seen displayed in museums and folk-art galleries. These days, recycling is aimed at reducing the volume of garbage that goes to landfills. In the thirties, it was a matter of survival.

Gladys McDonald, who grew up in Mortlach, Saskatchewan, never felt that she was poorly dressed during the depression thanks to her mother's skill with a sewing machine.

Though we weren't privileged to be able to wear designer jeans or fashion-labelled shirts and sweaters, we never wanted for warm clothes in winter or suitable garments for the hot summer months. My mother became an experienced seamstress. She performed miracles with outgrown or hand-me-down garments that were sent from relatives in Ontario or that came in boxes collected by the church. Our mother beamed with pride when a teacher commented that the children in our family were the best-dressed in school. Not only did my mother make our pyjamas, clothes for school, for play and for "Sunday best," she fashioned our overcoats for freezing temperatures and even found time to make some articles of clothing for children of single parents.

Joy Mitchell of Mitchellton, Saskatchewan, tells how her mother coped with clothing a family of five girls and a boy.

Mom was an excellent seamstress and made most of our clothes from other clothes that she ripped apart and remade. Dad's sister in England would send clothing they didn't need anymore. The clothes were beautiful but usually had to be altered. Mom made pretty dresses for us girls. Our panties were made from bleached flour bags and they wore like iron.

Many of the boxes of clothing that arrived on the prairies in the thirties were gathered and donated by the good people from eastern Canada. They arrived by train and were distributed either box by box, as they were in our district, or sometimes shared more practically, as Brownie Thiele, who grew up in Rock Glen, Saskatchewan, explains.

Our Eastern neighbours also sent huge bundles of used clothing! It was a red-letter day when those arrived. Our home was the distributing centre; neighbours came from all around to help sort and distribute. (Same when barrels of apples arrived.) It was a real social time. It took quite a while, with time out to visit and have lunch.

Most of the donated clothing was appropriate: men's trousers and jackets, children's wear, sweaters, overalls, socks, and occasionally shoes. Sometimes though, especially in districts where boxes were given out without the contents being checked, there were a few surprises.

Brownie Thiele was probably extremely pleased with the fancy dress she was allowed to wear to school. At least, she was until one stormy day.

One day I had gone to school as usual. I had one-and-a-half miles to walk. The wind began to rise and it worsened throughout the day. It was difficult to see the blackboard and writing was a gritty business. At home-time the dust storm was still raging. I got covered in dust; my hair was full of it, my arms and face grimy. When I was about a

Gladys McDonald (front, centre) and her brothers and sisters in the clothing made for them by their mother. *Gladys McDonald*

half-mile from home the wind died quite suddenly. It became very quiet and still. Then I heard thunder.

This particular day I was wearing a dress from one of the bundles from the east. It was a lovely dress, dark green, lace on the collar. It was made of a material called crepe de chene, not what would really be called a school dress, but I must have had fewer school clothes than church ones. Now crepe de chene shrinks when wet. It has to be restored to size by stretching and ironing, and at that, never regains its former glory.

Back to my walk home—the clouds opened and rain came down in buckets. In no time I was a sorry-looking mess, my hair full of mud, muddy streaks running down my face and arms. I got thoroughly soaked. And my lovely dress—it got shorter and shorter. At least I gave the family a good laugh when I arrived with my muddy face and mini-mini-mini skirt.

One of the more unusual items that arrived in one of our own family's boxes was a minister's black frock coat. It was in excellent condition and intricately tailored. One can only think that its original owner must have greatly increased in girth for it to be discarded. It was too small for Dad, and, anyway, a more unsuitable garment for a practical farmer could hardly be imagined. Mother decided to make me a coat from it. She carefully dismantled it—ripped out seams, and washed and pressed all the little bits that resulted. There seemed to be an awful lot of little pieces, none big enough to fit the parts of a pattern. Finally, by matching grain and sewing strips together she managed to get it cut and sewn. My little coat consisted of twenty-three separate pieces.

I remember distinctly one of our boxes. At least I remember the most distinctive thing about it. The box contained two frilly gauzy evening dresses, one blue, one green. No sleeves, just little spaghetti straps over the shoulders. Mom couldn't possibly remodel them into anything useful, but they sure came in handy when Carolie and I played "dress-up." We felt elegant and would even have worn them to church if we had been allowed to.

There is a joke—it can't be called an urban myth since it is more like a rural sneer—about Robin Hood peering out from the back of girls' bloomers that were made of flour sacks. Flour sacks and sugar bags figured large as raw material used in the thirties, but I saw very few that were not snowy white. I even remember the scrubbing with homemade lye soap and the boiling and bleaching that made them that way. When most bread was homemade, there were a lot of one-hundred-pound bags available, and bags were also sold for very little at nearby bakeries. Each provided a square yard of sturdy cotton. Sugar bags were of even better quality cotton.

Some of them were made into clothing—shirts, blouses, and underwear—but in our district, flour bags were mainly hemmed and used as dish towels, or flat felled together as bedsheets. Sugar-bag cotton was made into pillow cases, tea cloths, and even kitchen curtains. There was not much money for buying things of beauty in those days, but when these cotton bags were hemmed and then embroidered with flowers and leaves, they ended up both useful and pretty. (Embroidery cotton sold at 10 cents for three large hanks, each twice the size of the puny little ones we now pay 79 cents apiece for.)

One of the best things that happened in the thirties—at least for girls—was that pants became acceptable women's clothing for sports and outerwear. Maybe when skirts were ankle length and always had several layers of flannel petticoats beneath, legs didn't get chilblains, but I can tell you that a pair of stockings, even over long-legged underwear, does not do much to keep winter winds out. We didn't get the slim insulated pants that today's ski bunnies sport, but it was pretty nice to be able to stuff our skirts into warm baggy "skipants" and slip the suspenders over our shoulders before venturing out into snowbanks.

And aviator caps! Remember aviator caps? Mothers made close-fitting blanket cloth caps, lined with flannelette, that peaked down to cover the forehead and buttoned under the chin. Tie Grandma's Christmas present—a hand-knit scarf—around our necks, with a little slack to pull up over our mouths and noses if necessary, and we were ready for whatever winter dealt us.

John J. Molgat, who grew up at Ste. Rose Du Lac, Manitoba, has "warm" memories of the winter clothing of his day, although his aviator caps sound a bit more sophisticated than the ones we wore.

As today is the age of the astronaut, so ours was the dawn of aviation and the popular winter head-gear of boys my age was the "aviator cap," a fleece-lined, leather, skull-fitting cap, with ear flaps and straps held under the chin by a dome fastener. On either side there were circular perforations at ear level so that you could hear, but in order to keep the cold out of your ear-holes in bitter weather these could be closed off by flaps also equipped with dome fasteners. If left unfastened, these little flaps would stick out on either side of your head giving you the appearance of a surprised seal. The winter clothing of today is generally greatly superior to what was available then. Curiously enough, although the Eskimos must have been wearing them for centuries, the parka was unknown to us when I was a small boy, and between our aviator caps and our moccasins, most of us wore a heavy, lined, melton jacket called a mackinaw and corduroy breeches that disappeared into heavy long stockings coming up to our knees. Most of our garments were homemade, and in the absence of television, newspapers, or magazines, we were totally oblivious of fashion and accepted without question whatever our parents provided.

The onset of winter was marked by certain rituals that confirmed its arrival. One of these was the conversion, after a bath, from summer underwear to winter, fleece-lined combinations. Today's generation, brought up in warm houses, will probably have to ask grandparents for a description of this item of apparel. Although I have not worn them since that time, I still have fond memories of "the day of the change over," the feeling of soft cuddly warmth from ankles to neck as the combination wrapped itself around you. Being the oldest in the family had many drawbacks: I was forever cautioned to "set a good example for [my] little brothers," or urged to allow them this or that privilege because "they are smaller than you are." The Day of the Fleece Underwear brought compensation, because if the smallest brother had outgrown the hand-me-down from the previous year, these were discarded and all sizes shifted down one, leaving a vacancy at the top and I, the eldest, received a brand new set with fleece of maximum fuzzy softness.

As soon as the winter cold seemed to have set in permanently, we all went from felt boots covered with rubbers to moccasins with some bead-work that were made locally by an elderly Métis lady, and I can still recall my delight at the tawny brown colour and the pungent, smoky aroma of the deerskin tanned the Indian way.

When it was warm, my sister Carolie and I usually went bareheaded, but one summer Mrs. Lambert, our neighbour, who kept nine children warm and fed by miracles of ingenuity, showed Mother how to make sun hats. The head part was four triangles with curvy sides, sewed to fit the head, and there was a five-inch brim all around. The light cotton of the brim was kept from flopping in our faces by inserting a circle of haywire at the very edge. We tied ribbons under our chins to keep them from turning into kites when the wind blew—and it mostly did.

Now that I am a grandmother, I realize those sun hats gave my grandparents one of their lighter moments. One day on our way home from school Carolie and I went through Grandpa's yard and stopped off at their outdoor toilet. We don't remember now just who knocked the other's sun hat down the third hole, accidentally, but the other one then threw the remaining hat down in retaliation. Suddenly we realized we were both in serious trouble. So we told Grandma what we had done. Grandpa fished them out with the hoe, and Grandma cleaned them up and gave us a good scolding. They stood together behind the toilet, watching our progress through the pasture, and I am pretty sure they were laughing. They didn't tell on us either. Mom never found out until years later when we told her ourselves.

Making Ends Meet

O ne day when we were kids my sister and I were feeling very hard done by. Our cousin was to be married in Admiral, twelve miles away, and we couldn't go. A heavy April snowstorm had buried the roads so deeply that neither the Model T nor even the horses could get through. We kept pestering our dad who finally said, "Only if an aeroplane lands here and takes you." Shortly after that comment, an aeroplane did come into view and flew practically over the house. Carolie and I yelled and waved at it—but it just kept on going.

We are so blasé about aeroplanes nowadays. Every day jet trails make their spiderweb vapour trails across prairie skies. People around Moose Jaw hardly stop their work to watch the Snowbirds practise their aerobatics before returning to their base south of the city. It is still kind of a big deal for me to go to the airport and actually board a plane, travel to other parts of Canada and occasionally overseas. But it is not the big deal it used to be.

About twenty-five years ago, Cecil (Sonny) and Sadie Goddard came back to our Mitchellton district. He retired from the oil fields and decided to take over the farm his mother and father had homesteaded many years before. However, farming didn't take over his life. His heart was still in the clouds, as it had been since he was a lad. He made a landing strip in a field. He once built an aeroplane in his basement and practically had to dismantle it to get it up the stairs and outside. Every once in a while we saw him soaring overhead in his little red and white plane, looking over the countryside, just for fun. It all started in the 1930s and Cecil provides a good description of how the depression forced some people to turn to new ways of making a living.

You asked for something that turned out good regarding the great depression and at first I was sure that there was nothing good about it. I then remembered—I met and married a nice young lady, and I learned to fly an aeroplane, and I went to the far north to a gold mine. The north had no depression. Wages were as high as 75 cents an hour, not 5 dollars a month as in the south.

I had built a couple of aeroplanes and each could fly, but I was trying to teach myself to fly. The first flight was a disaster that demolished the crude plane. My mother was a schoolteacher. She had managed to save $60. Mother said, "Learn $60 worth. It is all I can spare!"

I went to Moose Jaw. My instructor was Dick Ryan, a World War I air force instructor. The plane was a Gypsy Moth. He sat in an open cockpit in front of me. Millions of grasshoppers darkened the sky at noon. Every time you came in to the hangar, you had to clean their remains from the leading edge of the wings and the propeller as they greatly reduced the plane's performance. Dick Ryan said, "You are catching on quick. In fact, I think you will break the club record for short dual time, which now stands at four hours, thirty minutes before solo flight." I had only four hours and ten minutes in when he climbed out and took his seat cushion with him. He stood at the wing tip and waved the cushion for me to go. I sort of felt there was one thing missing, a very necessary thing, like the instructor's head in the front cockpit! The head at the wingtip let fly a few quick words and I could read his lips. "Open that damn throttle, what the heck is the matter with you?"

I opened the throttle and a few minutes later landed beside him. He smiled and waved me into the air two more times. I had flown solo! But of course I still had no licence. Two years later, I got a letter from him saying that he would put me through for a licence for free, because I had learned so easily. He was sure that me and another young guy from Saskatoon would license in only twelve hours total flying time, as at that time the government gave the club $100 for each pilot they turned out. The nearly bankrupt flying club would get $200 from the government but it meant that we were "owned" by the military. About three years later war broke out. This would be the first war in history to be decided in the air. The government had kept track of all the early fliers and even offered to buy our grounded planes to be used to train mechanics. Thousands of men had to be trained to fly, bomb, navigate, and kill.

To get back to the depression, I was working in the garage at Pennant, Saskatchewan, for long hours and poor pay. Three of us young guys were reading about the gold and silver mines starting up at Goldfields and Yellow Knife. The mines were going to hire on, at Prince Albert. A kind old man named Axel Nelson had been listening to our lament and in his smooth Scandinavian voice he said, "I help you. You know I rolled my Plymouth and broke her up bad. You boys fix her up good again and I loan you the car and a tent and food and gas and you go to P.A. and hire on." He was wise, as I was shop mechanic and welder, Pop Bunis was a fine cabinet maker, and Delmar Yost was a good electrician and handy man. In ten minutes we had the wreck in the shop. We worked on it all night and in the morning Pop drove it to Axel's house and said, "Here she is." Axel was as good as his word.

We drove to P.A., and all three of us were hired on at different times. I was told to show up at the Canadian Airways float dock on the North Saskatchewan River in the city of Prince Albert. When a plane lit on the water, coming in from the north and the gold and silver, even on Sunday, the manager of the Hudson's Bay store and people from other stores were right there trying to sell them clothes. There were even barbers yelling, "Haircut— 35 cents!" That is how bad things were in the south. Work at the gold mines paid as much as 75 cents an hour while in the south a man could work twelve hours a day for $5 a month.

My plane came in and I told the pilot I could fly, in hope that he would put me beside him. He did do this and

Cecil Goddard and his first homemade plane. *Cecil Goddard*

he even let me fly the big bush plane. The plane was full
of carpenters and their big boxes of tools. I also noticed
that the red lines on the floats were under the water, so I
knew we were over-loaded. We taxied to the middle of the
river and turned west toward a bridge. She did not gain
speed fast like a land plane. She did gain some speed but I
knew she was not going to fly over the bridge and the hole
under the bridge did not look big enough for us to go
through, but it was. As she gained speed, tons of water was
flying from the floats. She left the water and slowly
climbed to eight thousand feet to get out of the smoke
from tremendous bush fires raging below us.

The company Fairchild 71 flew me from the gold mine
to a tent outcamp where I was put on a bull gang. A couple of weeks later the same plane landed. We all ran out to
the dock. The pilot yelled, "Is Goddard here?" I said,
"Yes," and then heard, "Goddard, roll your blankets and
get aboard now." He flew me to Goldfields, a town and a
mine for gold. I was given a cutting and welding torch.
At times I was flown to outcamps to repair machines,
machines that looked beyond repair. They just dumped a
man and a helper out with an acetylene outfit and welding

Cecil Goddard and friends, with Cecil's plane. *Cecil Goddard*

gas and said, "We will pick you up after you have that wreck going." I found it difficult to do the impossible, but it could be done. The cold in winter was beyond belief at times.

After two years I returned to the garage at Pennant and got married. When I look back honestly, this was the best thing to happen to me during the depression. My other pals came south too. They drifted to far away places.

War broke out. I was soon on military planes. The government's investment had paid off. They had a pilot with many hours that had only cost them $100. I trained men. The estimated cost of the instruction given to each member of the air force was $25,000 for pilots, $15,000 for navigators, and $10,000 for bomb-aimers.

I am now eighty-six years old, and I had a pilot's licence for over sixty years. I flew home-made planes for nearly fifty years. Some of the planes I made rest in museums, at Assiniboia and Mossbank, Saskatchewan, and two planes in Reynold's museum at Wetaskiwin, Alberta. One of the Reynold's planes now hangs in the Air Terminal building in Calgary. I would still be flying these planes only they took my flying licence from me because welding had damaged my eyes.

Very few of the "$100 pilots" are still alive. My great Irish instructor, Dick Ryan, died several years ago at age ninety-nine. Under his care the first scheduled flights of our oceans began, and today we can fly anywhere in the world.

Dick Ryan's students survived many years of flying because when landing we can still hear his voice. "You watch that air speed, it is getting near the stall. Keep the speed up." And for many thousands of landings—I kept the speed up.

RELIEF

Children of the thirties grew up to be the men and women, the citizen voters, and legislators of later years. Now we take for granted things like the old age pension, social services and welfare, even Canada pension—all the humanitarian measures initiated by those who endured the privation of depression. It is almost impossible for younger people to realize just how much attitudes have changed since the thirties when "going on relief" was about as low as one could get.

There are very few "rugged individualists" who now believe a man should sink or swim on his own, except maybe those whose personal fortunes are secure—and often inherited. Most of us pay our taxes reluctantly, but we know that some of it provides essentials of life for the unfortunate. There are still those who fall between the cracks, of course, but the general attitude now is "Let us fix that" rather than "Serves them right."

When I read local community history books, I find there was, in those hard times, a great difference in the way help was received. From the men and women who lived through those days, there is heartfelt gratitude expressed for the generosity of the good people in the east and in the west, who filled box cars with apples, cheese, beans, root vegetables, potatoes, and even salt cod; filled the box cars and sent them to people they didn't know, in places they would never see. The prairie people were grateful, but they were not surprised. Generosity is a part of prairie ethos. Relief "given" by the governments of the day was another matter entirely. It was given grudgingly, doled out after a humiliating application procedure, and the ensuing debt applied to the one thing prairie people valued most, their land. The apples, the cheese, even the salty fish—these were manna to a stricken heart. Government relief was a rasp to the soul.

As the number of families requiring direct relief in the form of money to buy food, clothing, and fuel increased, the problem of relief became the joint concern of municipal, provincial, and federal governments as early as 1929. In 1931 the Saskatchewan government set up the Relief Commission. Food and clothing for human needs and feed for livestock were distributed.

Historian John Archer, in his book *Saskatchewan: A History*, explains the action taken by governments of the day.

On September 22, 1930, the federal government passed The Unemployment Relief Act. This was a national measure that was too general and did not meet prairie farm needs. On August 25, 1931, the Saskatchewan government set up the Saskatchewan Relief Commission, which was to "relieve distress and provide employment." This helped a little but could not meet the overwhelming disaster that struck farm and city.

The Lake Johnstone and Sutton Municipalities history book, *Furrows and Faith*, has copied excerpts from the municipal council records that show the extent to which relief dominated the business of council in the 1930s.

January 1930: $8650 borrowed for relief purposes.

March 1930: thirty-five applications for relief feed approved and five applications for coal and flour approved.

April 1930: twenty applications for coal and flour approved and forty-nine applications for feed approved.

February 1931: ten applications for coal and flour and sixty-six applications for feed issued. Not more than $35 per quarter section was approved. People were to sign a note of consent for a lien to be registered against their land.

April 1931: applications for relief approved: forty for gas and oil, fifty-two for seed grain, six for feed, and four for hay.

May 1931: applications for relief approved: nine for food, ten for fodder, twenty-three for gas and oil, and fifty-three for seed grain.

May 1932: municipal mill rate set at seven mills on the dollar: four mills for administration, one mill for road maintenance, and two mills for interest on relief loans.

September 1934: work done to repay relief set at $2/day for a man, 75 cents/horse per day where absolutely necessary to use horses. Said work was to be done on telephone lines and roads, and if any person refused to work when he was asked to, his relief orders were to stop.

September 1935: application to the Voluntary Relief Committee made for vegetables for the R.M. All coal orders on local mines to be written at $2 per ton at the minehead.

November 1935: four persons paid a total sum of $19.50 towards their relief accounts. Sixteen families that had been refused food orders by the inspector received potatoes.

December 31, 1936: Relief Advances stood at $102,530 and Uncollected Taxes at $187,636.

September 1937: Council moved not to file Tax Enforcement liens for 1937.

June 1938: ten applications sent on to the Relief Committee for consideration since they were overlooked before. (Courtesy of the editor, Phyllis Zado)

It is evident that the local councillors were really in a bind. Their neighbours, often their own families, were in distress. Help was needed just to keep people warm and fed, to keep life in the cows, the chickens, the horses—the animals that provided food and a way to work the land. But the council was forced to pick and choose which friend or neighbour to help, and to enforce regulations about registering liens, working off taxes, and distribution, in order to be able to borrow the money needed. There was some bitterness, some allegations of favouritism aimed at the members of council, but being councillor wasn't the kind of a job that people were knocking down the doors to get, either. Pretty well everyone knew that council was doing the best it could under very difficult circumstances.

In the excerpt above for September 1934, there is mention made of requiring work on roads and telephone lines to pay off relief debt. Sounds so sensible and logical, doesn't it? Perhaps a personal note may clarify the subject.

Our family struggled through the early part of the 1930s without relief. However, after years of scarce crops and beggarly prices for what we could produce, Dad finally had to make application. At that time we were a family of five: Mother, Dad, girls age ten and seven, and a boy of two. To the best of my knowledge we eventually got $8 a month in the form of a voucher at the local grocery, and $20 in the fall to get winter clothing. The clothing allowance came as a voucher to Cooper's Department Store in Swift Current. When Highway #4 was being built from Val Marie to Swift Current, Dad took his best team and worked about ten miles north of Cadillac for two weeks, the amount of time he was permitted, as many farmers wanted to share in the work in order to reduce the amount charged against their land. His work boots were completely worn out, so he worked in his "church" shoes, and they were in tatters when he got home. Wages for himself and his team were applied against the debt incurred by receiving relief.

Mother took care of the chores and the family while he was away. She had two bags of oat chop and with that she had to feed the small flock of chickens, a pig, a cow, and Queen, our old mare who had a foal. Three days before Dad was due home, Queen collapsed in the barn. With the added stress of nursing the foal, she had starved on the meagre rations. Mom asked Grandpa to shoot her. He had no bullets so had to put her down with an axe blow to the head, and then with his team, he hauled the carcass away. Mother was frantic with guilt, but she had done the best she could under the circumstances.

Monetary relief vouchers were handled with many strings attached, and there was such a stigma in applying for relief at all that it really was a choice of last resort. It is no surprise that people so treasured the box cars of fruit, vegetables, beans, and fish. This food was seen as an outpouring of generosity, generosity that could and would be repaid if the need ever occurred. In a way this was not altogether fair to the "powers that were" of the time. I did not know until recently that some of the food had been paid for at its source by the Relief Commission, and was shipped for free by the CPR. However, I am sure that nobody made a fortune selling it and probably even sold much of it at a loss. The bargains between farmers who produce and government that disposes won't have changed that much, not even in seventy years.

Margaret Hamilton, who lived near Mazenod, Saskatchewan, wrote in the reminiscences of her life, *Something To Remember*, a description of the arrival of the box cars from the east and west.

The relief cars coming into every little town from other provinces were a God-send, even giving us a lesson in Christian charity, as priest, minister, and the inevitable "grabbers" tried to evolve a system of fair distribution. From the eastern provinces came clothes and home-canned produce. The most delicious jam of my experience was a quart of homemade black currant jam from Ontario. British Columbia sent box cars of apples, thrown in loose, like grain. By the time the men-folk had used scoop-shovels to fill their sacks, the damage was pretty extensive. However, the damaged ones were quickly eaten or canned as applesauce, while the sound ones were carefully put away to be kept as long as hungry children could make them last. Thousands of them found their way into school lunch boxes, often rationed to half an apple per head. One neighbour, looking at a bowl of the choicest ones with new eyes, remarked, "Who would cook such beautiful apples!" Of course, from a nutritionist's point of view she was right, too. From down east came box cars of long dried fish and cheese and beans, wonderful protein foods, but "whether" or "what" to do with those discoloured, unappetizing flaps of fish was a matter for debate and discussion. They would have made good shingles or durable shoe soles! Nevertheless, by soaking and trimming, and doctoring with a good parsley sauce, they were gratefully eaten by the majority. Potatoes came in car-loads, too: many of them, alas! in the winter, so

A Bennett buggy is perhaps the most well-known symbol of ingenuity in the face of hardship from the dirty thirties. *Saskatchewan Archives Board/S-B 7114*

that no matter how well covered in the sleigh or how fast the horses were driven home, some were bound to freeze before they got down cellar. All were gratefully received, just the same!

Harvey Haug, who lived near Outlook, Saskatchewan, remembers the days when relief cars of food came to their district.

People really didn't have any money during the worst years. A lot in our neck of the woods got what they called "relief." I suppose now-a-days it would be called "Social Assistance." Not quite the same though because we weren't given money. However, car loads of food, animal fodder, and such came by rail from the east and was distributed to families. The food included wheels of cheese, large slabs of dried salted codfish, beans, apples, and root vegetables. We never did go hungry. Fodder for the animals was also much appreciated.

Joy Mitchell, of Mitchellton, Saskatchewan, remembers the coming of the railroad relief cars, too.

Another big highlight was when the relief car would arrive. We received fruit and vegetables. There were also chunks of salt codfish—and I loved it. When cooked properly it was delicious, especially when it was smothered in a cream sauce and served on toast. The apples were of several varieties. We had fun tasting and eating them. The vegetables were also good. We learned to eat most of them. I had never liked turnips or parsnips before, but I soon acquired a taste for them, too.

Brownie Thiele, who grew up in Rock Glen, Saskatchewan, describes how grateful prairie people were for the food that was sent from eastern Canada.

Living on a farm as we did, we never went hungry as many in the cities did. We had pigs, chickens, cattle and their products as well as some garden, although in some years the garden didn't amount to much. My mother was an excellent cook and could make a meal out of very little. In this connection, our Good Samaritan neighbours from Ontario and Nova Scotia helped considerably. Barrels of apples and vegetables came from the east. I can still smell the delicious odour when a barrel of apples was opened— and the wonderful flavour. We also received dry, salted codfish from Nova Scotia. Stories and jokes about how to cook the fish abounded. One "recipe" said to nail the fish to a board, soak everything in a pot of water for a few days and then boil for several hours. Take out, remove fish from board, throw the fish away and eat the board! Not so in our house—my mother, after a bit of experimenting, served many a tasty dish of codfish.

There is a sort of ironic codicil to the story of relief and the debt it put on the land. My dad and many others scrimped, made do, and endured until they could no longer justify the deprivation their families were suffering before undergoing the humiliation of applying for relief. When times improved, the first thing they did was to pay off that debt. This came before new clothing and equipment, before anything not absolutely essential. When the land was debt free, they could relax. Others, often those who were first to apply, were not so uptight. About a year and a half after Dad's farm was lien free (I would like to say "home free"), the Canadian government declared a moratorium on all remaining relief debts.

PESTS, SMALL AND SMALLER

Moses had it right. If you are looking for a plague to demoralize the countryside—go for locusts—grasshoppers, that is. Apparently they are the same insect. It is just that when grasshoppers multiply past their food supply, they stop acting like individuals. They migrate as hordes and are called locusts.

I remember days when we trooped out of school to eat our noon lunch on the shady north side of the school and looked sky-ward to locate the source of the dry raspy chittering that got louder minute by minute. It was the noise of millions of grasshopper wings. Locust wings. Locusts came from the south so thick that clouds of them dimmed the blazing sunlight. And when they descended to the ground they destroyed everything green that grew. They were so terrible, that in a queer way, they were almost magnificent.

There wasn't much that anyone could do about clouds of locusts. However, newly hatched grasshoppers in the sod verge around the edge of newly seeded fields were another subject. In a matter of days they could move into the field and turn the green shoots of emerging grain into brown sterile ground. Farmers kept track of their maturation, and when the insects were ready to move in, the men would go out early in the morning and spread damp sawdust laced with paris green, a type of arsenic, all around the edge of the new crop. The hoppers, who were avid for moisture, dined on the damp sawdust and died of the arsenic. It was not much of a solution, and often didn't help, but it was the only way farmers had to try to pro-tect their crops. There were no sprays and no sprayers in those days. Occasionally, flocks of gulls would appear, almost like a miracle. They cleaned up the fields and disappeared as myste-riously as they had come.

Jean Freeman, now of Regina, Saskatchewan, recently heard about that kind of miracle.

I was born in 1934, on the day (as I found out fifty years later) of the worst onslaught of grasshoppers that southern Saskatchewan ever endured! Trains couldn't move on the tracks because the drive wheels mushed the grasshoppers and just slipped on the rails. The grasshoppers ate everything on the clotheslines, my mother told me later, and flew into people's eyes, noses, and mouths if they ventured outside. Then, it rained and the sewers were clogged with grasshoppers. But miraculously, a vast flock of Franklin's gulls appeared and gorged themselves on the grasshoppers, and the plague was over. But this is supposed to be about happy stories of the thirties, right? Well, I suppose the part about the gulls was happy, when you come to think of it.

About the only defence the prairie population had was humour. Postcards of what looked like an actual snapshot of an immense grasshopper roped onto a railway car were sent to far-away friends. We farm kids told our town cousins how good the grasshopper drumsticks were, especially when fried in butter. We would grab a grasshopper by the wings, look it in the eye, and chant, "Spit grasshopper, spit tobacco juice, or I will pull your head off." It always spit, so we didn't pull off its head. We just stomped on it instead.

When the moisture-craving insects wreaked havoc on freshly washed clothing hung out on the clothesline by chomping little holes here and there to get to the damp part, it wasn't considered all that funny. The hoppers didn't distinguish between rinse water and perspiration. From the Rock Glen, Saskatchewan, area, Brownie Thiele draws this memory.

The grasshoppers came in clouds, billions of them. They darkened the sun! Looking up they seemed to be so very high. The sun glinted off their wings making silvery flashes. I suppose there was some beauty in that sight—

Engraving of a swarm of grasshoppers approaching a homestead. *Glenbow Archives/NA-2426-11*

I still remember it clearly. One day my brothers and my dad were hauling green oat sheaves. Toward mid-morning my brother hung his denim jacket on a fence post. In late afternoon, work done, he picked up his jacket. All he had in his hand was the collar, cuffs, front fasteners, and heavier seams. The rest was hole upon hole—chewed up by the grasshoppers.

Army worms came true to their name, marching in a straight line. They came from the west in a column about sixteen feet wide. When they got to our house they crawled up the west side, across the roof and dropped off the east side. Our door was on the east side, and it was a tricky business getting outside without getting a worm down your neck.

They continued on eastward in a straight line toward our coulee where the well and the watering trough were. When the worms reached the trough, they climbed up, fell in, and drowned. When enough had drowned to make a platform, the rest were able to march across, up the other side and down to earth again, still in a straight line. Before the animals could drink the troughs had to be emptied, scoured, and refilled.

In places where the worms crossed roads, it was like driving in greasy slippery mud. The ground they crossed looked as if it had been cultivated—not a blade of anything was left. The only good thing about army worms was that they did not stay long. It took about twenty-four hours for them to pass over our land.

In the district where I grew up, most of the farmers came from the conifer forests of Norway via the deciduous forests of Minnesota, or at least their ancestors had. I sometimes thought they were so "into" planting trees around our district because of some sort of folk-urge, an unconscious wish to go back home where trees were tall and winds were tempered. Anyhow my grandpa and my dad both kept planting and replanting trees as long as they farmed. All across the prairie, south of the "bush" country, there are little clumps of trees that mark where settlers anchored their dreams of a brighter future by planting poplars, elms, maples, caraganas, and lilacs around their yards. It is surprising, even in these days when giant farm machines need larger and larger fields, that so many of these relics of faded dreams are still cultivated around rather than rooted out. Perhaps in every prairie heart there is a taboo on destroying a tree.

The first homesteaders didn't lament the lack of trees when they were breaking their fields. Many who had come from parts of the world where tree-chopping and root-digging were the major part of "making land" thought themselves very fortunate. Their building sites were often placed on top of a hill, the better to see and be seen, especially as neighbours were not especially plentiful. It wasn't too long before they realized that a tree or two to break the wind would be a great comfort.

When the drought and wind-driven sand of the thirties killed off the less hardy of shelterbelt trees, the caragana came into its own. A native of the Siberian steppes, it clung to life, even flourished, where other trees gave up the ghost. It became the tree of choice to plant around the outside of a yard. Sometimes, in the lee of a sturdy caragana hedge, poplars, maples, elms, and ash trees managed to survive. In its shade, chickens made hollows to dust their feathers, the dog rested after chasing imaginary intruders, his tongue dripping, out of breath and panting. The children sat out of the sun, picking the yellow pealike flowers and biting the base to get a hint of honey, or later in summer, cracking the pods and eating the still green seeds. They didn't taste all that good, but that is what kids did with caragana pods.

The Excel history book tells how the citizens of Ormiston, Saskatchewan, defied the drought.

Present day residents of Ormiston owe a grateful "thank you" to the hard working Board of Trade of the twenties and thirties for the beauty that is theirs to enjoy. In the middle thirties, when the drought was at its worst, these men, headed by D. J. McKay, planted poplars, Manitoba maples, and elms on this sandy site. They were laughed and jeered at by some for having the audacity to think any trees would grow in this sand pile during these rainless years. But these men with vision planted, watered and cajoled—and lo, the trees did grow! Cooperative citizens did their part by giving these hardy, courageous treelings tender care. They saved, carried and begged water for them; it is rumoured even going without baths themselves, to water their trees. Those of them who still live here, and those who return to visit, know how well their efforts were rewarded when they walk down our tree-lined streets on a summer day.

Another insect pest of the prairies chomped its way through the trees and shrubs that came into existence through the sheer determination of settlers. Does anyone else remember the year of the Cecropia moth? A relative of the silkworm moth, it invaded our area in about 1934. South winds must have blown a batch of them in because they are not native here. All of a sudden the maple trees east of our house were full of little green worms with hairy red, yellow, orange, and blue warts on their backs. Little warty green worms turned into big warty green worms as the leaves disappeared from the maples. They got pretty big for worms—over three inches long and as big around as a man's thumb. The caterpillars spun cocoons in the nearly leafless trees, and several weeks later the moths, with a four or five inch wing span, appeared. They were beautiful—purple and silvery grey, with mauve eye spots and feathery antennae. But, beautiful though they were, that did not make up for the damage to our trees. The stress of defoliation added to the drought and sand storms killed the maples. In 1936, Dad spent several days pulling out the roots with a team of horses, a logging chain, and an axe. The next spring he planted new little trees, but 1937 was not the year for that, so it wasn't until the early forties that we again had trees east of the house.

As for the moths—they just disappeared. I guess our climate was too much for them. I saw a straying Cecropia moth on our screen door last summer. As beautiful as it was, it only brought back memories of those warty green worms eating up our maples.

As we speed down the highways, I hope we never get too rushed to notice the little green clumps of trees here and there on the prairie. They are such a testament to the faith and perseverance of our parents and grandparents, who tried to make their homes a pleasant place to live. And I hope practicality always yields to sentiment so that those little patches of green remain standing in memory of the men and women who dreamed dreams and planted trees.

Madge Bennett of Moose Jaw recalls yet another "pest" that prairie farmers were not particularly fond of. In the Coronach area of Saskatchewan, residents devised rabbit drives that were social as well as practical community events.

When I taught in the Coronach area, some of the farmers had a rabbit drive every fall. The country is quite flat, and at that time, nothing seemed to grow in the fields but Russian thistle. There were always a lot of jack rabbits, so on some Saturday after harvest, the neighbours would all gather on one farm. They formed a long line, some on horseback and others walking. Everyone was warmly dressed as there could be frost on the ground, and they also had to protect themselves from the prickly thistles they walked through. It was a cheerful group, a lot of talking back and forth, and some of them even sang and yelled to scare the rabbits.

The idea was to herd them toward a winged corral made of wire. The corral was ten or twelve feet high and sometimes covered to keep the rabbits from jumping out. When they were rounded up they were killed and sent to the fox farms.

After the tiring walk, the farmer whose land had been cleared of the pests invited everyone to have lunch, coffee and sandwiches, or sometimes baked beans or stew. There was a lot of socializing and catching up on the news before everyone left for home.

A pest that was more of a perennial bother (and seems to have become a symbol of the prairies) was the prairie gopher. Its proper name is "Richardson's ground squirrel," but you won't find many farmers who consider it a squirrel. Squirrels live in trees and eat nuts and don't bother people. I know the relationship but prefer to ignore it, too. I have never been able to figure out why I think squirrels are cute and gophers aren't. They both squeak, both have kind of bushy tails and prominent overbites, both can disappear in half a second. Maybe it has to do with my farmer genes.

There have been gophers on the prairie since prairie began. Gophers are "prairie" critters, "way-out-on-the-prairie" critters. And for centuries, way out there, hawks, badgers, foxes, and coyotes kept them thinned out. Settlement added farmers to the mix, farmers who planted tender grain every spring, who shot the hawks, badgers, coyotes, and foxes that occasionally varied their customary gopher diet with chicken dinners. Gophers flourished. The war began.

The big gun in the war was gopher poison. Municipalities sold cans of strychnine-based liquid that was mixed with grain, one canful to a gallon pailful of wheat or oats. Men, women, and older children walked the fields, pail in one hand, spoon wired to a long lath in the other, and placed a small spoonful of poison grain in each burrow, deep enough that a stray cow or calf could not sample it. Often dead gophers were seen on the return trip, but sometimes the victims died after crawling back into their burrows so it was hard to judge how effective the poison was. One of our neighbours was dissatisfied with the strength of our municipality's offering. He offered to eat some to prove his case, and although nobody called him on it, he did chew up and swallow several kernels of the poison-saturated grain. His later opinion: "Oh, I got a bit of a belly ache, but it didn't kill me!"

In his book *Saskatchewan: A History*, John Archer reports that the gopher "wars" didn't start in the thirties.

The emphasis placed on food production for the war effort (World War I, 1914–1918) led to a campaign to eradicate gophers. Prizes were awarded for the most gophers destroyed by a school. On May 1, 1917, a "gopher day" was declared, and 980 schools reported that more than half a million gophers had been exterminated. The remaining gophers, however, simply went about their business of multiplying with undiminished zeal.

Municipalities often put bounties on gophers, sometimes a cent a tail. But in early spring before the litters of young were born, or old enough to survive on their own, the bounty was sometimes doubled or tripled. Pity the fellow who had to count the tails. He was handed sealed tobacco cans or lard pails full of ripe mementoes, and his count had to tally with the donor's expectations. You may be sure that any kid who brought in gopher tails had made his own count, and in his mind had probably spent the resulting riches several times.

Joy Mitchell, of Mitchellton, Saskatchewan, and her family made good use of the gopher tail bounty.

We would help Dad poison gophers. The next day we would go and pull off the tails and put them in a can. When we had a can full we would take it to the Municipal office where we would get 5 cents per tail if we brought them in May. After that the price went down. We would take the money and get something we needed as 5 dollars went a long way in those days.

Snaring gophers was a universal skill among farm kids of the thirties. Any of us could rummage around the edge of a straw stack, retrieve a couple of lengths of twine, and make a noose. Then, equipped with an old syrup or lard pail (or in emergencies even a lunch pail) to carry water from a nearby pump, water trough, or slough, the hunt was on. A burrow with dirt that looked freshly disturbed was selected, and the noose was patted into place a couple of inches from the top. Gophers usually have a couple of back doors to their burrows so these had to be plugged. Then one kid knelt on the uphill side of the hole, the end of the twine at the ready in his hand. His accomplice carefully poured water past the noose—a steady small stream—not so much as to dislodge the noose but enough to suggest to a rodent that there might be a better place, a drier place, somewhere else. As soon as the gopher's head emerged, the twine holder struck; a quick snap of the wrist and several swings around his head and a couple of hearty thumps on the ground made for a quick and merciful dispatch, especially compared to death by strychnine.

Jean Freeman writes:

I remember spending barefoot afternoons in my grandma's back pasture with my aunt (only a few years older than I was) drowning out gophers so we could get the bounty on their tails! Was it a penny apiece or as much as 2 cents or a nickel? I can't remember now, but I do remember that it was very hard work, hauling pails of water from the barn tank, and guarding the "back door" of the gopher's burrow so he couldn't escape. And mercenary creatures (perhaps with soft hearts though) that we were, when we did catch a gopher, we always amputated the tail and let the little critter go, because we had been told that they grew their tails back! Bounty hunting was lots of fun in those days too!

There were a lot of escapades connected with gopher hunting that never made it to parents' ears, according to Dorothy Gessell of Strasbourg, Saskatchewan.

One day Mother dressed eighteen-month-old Donald and put him in our little wagon. She told the older boys to look after him while she was busy. They had planned to go drowning gophers. They could earn one cent for every gopher tail at the municipal office. Donald was pulled in the wagon across the prairie, until they found some gopher holes with a small slough nearby. The snare was set and water poured into the hole. One brother had the string in hand, ready for the catch.

"Look out, I got him!" Kenneth yelled as the gopher tried in vain to break free. During the ensuing excitement, Donald fell out of the wagon and ended up in the edge of the slough. He screamed in protest. The two brothers rushed to rescue him. The gopher was forgotten.

The boys took Donald to the hill top where they stripped him. They put their jackets around him and spread his clothes out on the grass to dry. When they were dry, they re-dressed him and went back home. Mother and Dad were not told of this event until their twenty-fifth anniversary. Everyone present enjoyed a good laugh.

A few decades after the thirties, my ten-year-old son and his pal decided to snare gophers in our pasture. They found the syrup pail, the twine, a slough, and lots of gopher holes but had no luck. They asked me for technical advice. So at the age of forty-one, I supervised selecting an occupied burrow, blocking the back doors, and positioning the twine noose. I held the end of the twine as I advised them how to pour the water past the noose. All of a sudden the gopher's head appeared. You know what they say about learning to ride a bicycle—it works snaring gophers, too. I snapped the noose tight, swung the whole works around my head and slammed it onto the ground before you could say "Jack Robinson." (Well! That was the 1930s expression!) I do not think, in all my days as teacher, parent, and grandparent, I have ever had a more impressed audience. I went back to the house and left the boys to practise.

"Quit while you are ahead" is my motto.

Costco? I Don't Think So!

I wonder if anyone in the "baby-boomer" generation or younger realizes just how basic food production was in the 1930s. Talk about a "cottage industry"! We really got down to the nitty-gritty—everything from planting gardens; fighting off the weeds and bugs; harvesting the vegetables, canning peas, beans, and corn; pickling cucumbers, onions, tomatoes, and cauliflower; making cabbage into sauerkraut; manufacturing our own ice cream; to, of course, finding a cool, dark place to store the potatoes and turnips.

Every spring afternoon, when we picked the eggs, we kids were on the lookout for "broody" hens. They were the ones who wouldn't get off the nest when we came around, but instead were quite irascible, and even pecked at our wrist when we tried to get the eggs they were sitting on. They occasionally even drew blood! If there were a dozen fertile eggs handy, a broody hen was segregated in her own little hovel and given the clutch of eggs to "brood." After being kept warm for three weeks, they hatched out, and the old hen taught the chicks to scratch around for food, kept watch for hawks that might grab them, and kept them warm under her wings at night until they lost their baby down and became half-feathered teenagers, not very attractive but finally able to fend for themselves.

The pullets (the young females) were destined to be kept as replacements for the old hens whose egg-laying days were coming to an end. The nearly grown roosters were considered fair game to be caught, beheaded, defeathered, excavated, and cut into serving size to be fried up in butter—and if you think KFC is good, you should have been around when we had fried chicken for supper! After the young hens started laying, usually late in the fall, the day came when the senior ladies would be turned into roast chickens, and the ones that weren't roasted were canned. There are several generations now living who have never enjoyed home-canned chicken. It is a pity, but don't bother trying the commercially canned ones—they do not compare.

Of course, in the days before pressure cookers, canning meat or vegetables was risky because of the danger of botulism. A lot of care was taken to have everything clean and do the job properly. All vegetables and meat were processed in vigorously boiling water for at least four hours. When cool, the jars were tested to make sure they had sealed, and if one hadn't, you could bet on what was going to be served for supper. Jars of home-canned fruit, meat, and vegetables were kept in a cool, dark place. Any discolouration or odd odour upon opening was reason to discard the contents in some place even the animals couldn't get at it. In spite of the threat of food poisoning, I can't remember hearing about anyone who got sick from home-canned meat or vegetables, although I am sure there were some who did.

Every fall when the nights got frosty, butchering season rolled around. There were usually a couple of uncles to help out when Dad butchered, but every once in a while we kids got drafted into helping, too. We quite enjoyed it. Nothing is too gory for kids, I guess. We still butcher deer in the fall, but take it to Moose Jaw to be cut and wrapped. Everything had to be done at home, then, so for the next several days, there was a lot of cutting, chopping, cooking, curing, canning, and hard work for everybody. It was a great help if the weather was cold enough to freeze great chunks of beef. It could be thawed and either roasted or cut into steaks and chops when needed. Dad had a couple of spike nails on the north side of the house that were sturdy enough to hold quite a few pounds of fresh frozen beef. Hams and slabs of bacon were cured with a special salt, smokine, and salt peter mixture, wrapped in a piece of old sheeting, then frozen and buried in the oat bin. I think the idea was to keep the meat at an even below-zero temperature and also have it deep enough in the grain to discourage mice who might be inclined to chomp on the edges.

And how wonderful to have your own milk, butter, cream, cheese, and buttermilk. Just go out and get it from the cow.

Uh-huh. Every farm had several milk cows. A cow produces milk to feed her new calf, and a farmer intercepts the process by taking part of the milk for his family, removing the cream and feeding the calf on what is left over. Cows were timed to freshen, or to have their calves, at different times throughout the year so that there was at least one cow producing milk at all times. This is not quite as simple as it sounds. Wild animals have breeding seasons and usually produce young in the early spring. Man has manipulated the nature of domestic cattle for thousands of years so that cows are now able to bear young at any time of the year. A farmer must see that his animal is bred about nine months before her milk is needed, and just anytime will not do. She has to be "in heat," the two or three day period in a month when pregnancy is possible. (A by-product of raising calves, colts, piglets, and chickens was that, although there was then a prissy disinclination to speak of anything as vulgar as human reproduction, especially in front of young people, there were not too many surprises in store for kids who grew up on a farm.)

Having fresh whole milk morning and night sounds pretty handy. It too involved a lot of work. Not only did the cows have to be brought in from the pasture, they had to be watered and given a bit of oat-chop to keep them busy while being milked. Milking cows is a job replete with hazards—everything from being switched across the back of the neck with a hairy tail or being kicked while in a very precarious position to having to grab your milkpail and get out of the way if the cow decides it is time to relieve herself. When the milk is finally taken to the house, it has to be put through the cream separator, enough milk kept to feed the family, the cream put someplace cool, and the rest of the milk taken back to the barn to feed calves or pigs. (Actually the most annoying part of separating was washing all the little bits and pieces of the machinery; there seemed to be about forty pieces, and each one was just a bit slimier than the last. Getting everything put back together again was not hard except that one had to make sure that all the disks were kept in the same sequence they had been in when the process started.)

Cream was churned into butter—temperature was very important, too cold and the butter wouldn't "come," too warm and the butter was oily and hard to clean. Any extra cream was sent to the nearest creamery, and the cream cheque often took care of a good part of the grocery bill. Sour milk was often made into cottage cheese. My mother tried several times to make cheddar cheese with new milk. She filled the copper wash boiler, got the milk to lukewarm temperature, added dissolved rennet tablets, and when it "curded" cut the curds into little blocks with a wire stove-top toaster that looked like a grill. After a bit of stirring, the mix was strained and the block of curd put into a press. When it was firm, the block was put into a salt brine for several days, and then put in a cool place to "age." I don't know if Mom's concoction would ever have turned into cheddar cheese because we always ate it long before it got to the "aged" state. It tasted pretty good, but it wasn't cheddar!

Mention "ice house" today and the words evoke anything from igloos to the temporary crystal palaces northern Europeans build for sensation-seeking tourists. It wasn't always such an exotic phrase. We had an ice house when I was a kid. A lot of people did. Ours was a shed-roofed building, ten by twelve feet, with shingled walls and a two-foot-square trap door in the floor. People needed somewhere to store their farm-raised perishables. No side-by-side or walk-in fridges and freezers in those days.

Late every fall Dad used his team of horses to pull the ice house away from its place in the yard so that the dirt cellar beneath it could be cleaned out. After the ice on Haakenson's dam got to be about fifteen inches thick, neighbours gathered there with low-sided bobsleighs, ice saws, and tongs. They sawed the ice into foot-wide strips and broke the strips into chunks that were pulled out of the water with the tongs, and then loaded the blocks onto the sleighs. At home, the blocks were put into the open cellar, with dry sawdust spread under, over, and between the layers, both for insulation and to keep the blocks from freezing together in unre-movable chunks. Then the ice house was moved back over the hole and banked up ready to resist the heat of the coming summer.

The same sort of thing happened commercially in cities and large towns, on a vastly greater scale. Those were the days of ice-boxes and biffies; electricity and water were not yet universal amenities. Winter's chilly treasure was distributed by the "ice-man," just as milk and cream were distributed by the "milk-man."

As far as a lot of us were concerned, the best part of having an ice house on the farm was homemade ice cream. We had an "ice-cream freezer." The outside was a wooden bucket—constructed of upright three-quarter-inch-thick wooden staves held in place with three metal hoops. A hole about halfway up the side provided exit for the salty brine as the ice melted. The "tinned" inside container was centred on the bottom by a knob and socket. The "agitator" actually just stayed put, its wooden baffles scraping the freezing mix from the can sides as the can was turned by gears. The gears were nested in the clamp that spanned the top, and were connected to the handle.

Making ice cream was more a family project than a chore. Dad had to take a tub and hatchet, go down the hole in the ice house floor and get the ice. The sawdust was rinsed off and then we kids smashed the ice into wee bits in a burlap bag, or gunny sack as it was generally called. Meanwhile, in the kitchen, Mom made up the mix of cream, milk, sugar, beaten eggs, and flavouring. The tinned inside container could only be filled about two-thirds full because the mix expanded as it froze. The fully assembled freezer was taken to a shady spot outside the house and the space between the canister and the bucket packed with a mix of chopped ice and coarse salt. Even the littlest family member could turn the handle at first, but as the mixture started to freeze, we older children spelled each other off. When it was finally declared "frozen," Dad drained off the brine, removed the beater (everyone got a pre-taste of what clung to it), reassembled the lid and clamp, and repacked the bucket with fresh ice and salt. The whole works was covered with an old blanket and allowed to "set" until feast time arrived.

Because it was such a family project, making ice cream was usually reserved for a sunny Sunday afternoon. (Field work was seldom done on Sundays, a custom that I wish could be renewed.)

Often several families of aunts, uncles, and cousins would come to visit after church, and of course, everyone stayed for supper. Hard on the cook, but it evened out, as the next couple of Sundays everyone would meet at someone else's place, and that aunt would be chief cook. About 4:30 everybody helped carry fried chicken, potato salad, buns, coffee, lemonade, dishes, and utensils down to a little space in the trees that sister Carolie and I had cleaned out and called "Blackbird Park." We filled our plates from the bounty set out on the rickety table, sat around on old blankets to eat, and finished off the feast with bowls of creamy white ice cream.

One year in June, when cash was even more scarce than usual, the people responsible for the Boule Creek school picnic decided to forego the usual booth of candy bars and pop. Instead, any family that could, brought their freezer full of homemade ice cream, and others provided a mix of squeezed lemon juice, finely sliced lemon rind, and sugar to make lemonade. Prizes for races were little pieces of paper that we could trade for extra ice cream or lemonade.

Sugar Loaf school district near the little siding of Galilee, south of Moose Jaw, Saskatchewan, put on picnics that included ice cream, too, recalls June Mitchell.

Picnics were held in a nice spot on the prairie. Ice-cream was made in freezers with donated cream and ice from the Reis's ice house. That ice house had been dug into the ground, covered with a sod hut, and filled with ice in March. The ice lasted all summer. Men and boys turned the freezers. Ice-cream was free to all. Sometimes we had cones, a gift from the store keeper.

At the picnic we had races for all ages, with donated prizes. The ball games were on a diamond marked out on the grass, with bases made of gunny-sacks filled with sods. Good fielders developed during these games, as there was only one baseball, one softball, and one bat. If a ball was lost, that was the end of the ball-game!

Of course, not all ice cream was home made. Every little town had a "confectionery," usually a Chinese restaurant, that served dishfuls of ice cream to the diners and cones to the kids. It was far more of a treat then than it is now when everyone has a gallon of it in the freezer in the basement. In those days, an ice cream cone cost a nickel. And even when the newest fad came to our town, a double-header cone that took two scoops of ice cream to make, it still cost only a nickel! And if by some miracle, you got tired of vanilla ice cream, you could get chocolate or maple walnut flavour instead.

Joy Mitchell, of Mitchellton, Saskatchewan, and her family used to make a trip to town every Saturday. The excursion always involved an ice cream treat.

On Saturday night, Mom would dress us up, and Dad would hook the horses to the buggy. We would drive into Mitchellton where we could buy ice cream cones. (They cost only 5 cents.) We really took our time eating them and would see who could keep theirs the longest. The main reason for the trip was so Mom could bring in eggs and butter to trade for groceries, but as far as we children were concerned, the ice cream was the most important.

John J. Molgat, who grew up in Ste. Rose Du Lac, Manitoba, remembers ice cream in a different setting, when health measures were sort of handled on a wholesale basis.

A surgical team arrived and set up examination and operating rooms and recovery wards in the upper floors of the convent. War had been declared on tonsils and we were processed in batches—at least they used chloroform. When you woke up in the large dormitory room, surrounded by fellow sufferers you were given a dish of genuine store bought ice cream before being sent home. REAL ice cream, as opposed to the kind your mother made and which I now know to have been much superior, was then available only in the cafe operated by the Yee brothers. Bananas were likewise then viewed as a rare and exotic fruit, again for a long time procurable only at the Chinese cafe, where a 4 or 5 foot long bunch of them was suspended from a hook in the ceiling. The agonizing decision every Sunday was how to invest the weekly 5 cent allowance in such a way as to provide maximum satisfaction to the palate: a dish of ice cream or a banana? The bananas were at a fixed price of 5 cents each regardless of size and every time I had the funds to get one, I fervently hoped that Charlie, Pete, or Sam, whichever one of the brothers was behind the counter, would reach for one of the larger ones.

Speaking of "desserts," one of the heroes of the 1930s has to be rhubarb. Everybody had a couple of rhubarb plants in their garden patch. It was tough. Even when the man of the family accidentally tilled right through it in the initial spring cultivation, it came back, green and sour as could be. Later on, redder, less tart varieties of the plant were developed, but the rhubarb of the 1930s was the only kind we knew. It was the base for many desserts—rhubarb pie, rhubarb betty (a take-off on apple betty, baked with lots of sugar and sweet crumbs on top), and of course canned rhubarb sauce. It is a good thing sugar was relatively cheap then. Rhubarb was also an "extender." The idea was if one had a handful of strawberries, not enough for a family meal, cook them up with a bunch of rhubarb and the whole thing tasted like strawberries. Well, that was the idea, but in my experience all that happened was that the whole thing tasted like rhubarb! Rhubarb was also used to extend Saskatoons, peaches, and almost any other fruit. (And it all tasted like rhubarb to me!) Rhubarb is not actually a fruit, as the part used is the fleshy stem of the plant. The immense leaves contain a poison, oxalic acid, and were discarded. (We kids used them as parasols, occasionally, and now I hear the leaves can be made into a mush in a blender, diluted with water and used as an organic spray for bugs. Oh well, we didn't have blenders, anyway.)

Another free and staple fruit that was canned as well as eaten raw or made into jelly was the Saskatoon berry. Harvey Haug, who lived near Outlook, Saskatchewan, remembers:

A good homemade lunch for the haymakers, made without any of the modern conveniences we are so accustomed to these days. *Eleanor Kopperud*

Berry picking was also considered a big event. We would pack a lunch and take off to the sand hills east of Swanson. We travelled by wagon and horses. Our aunt and uncle always went as well. There was always a race to see who could pick and can the most Saskatoons. We had to travel with horses because in those years Dad had to jack the truck up on blocks because he couldn't afford either the gasoline or the licence.

But they were good times. It is too bad that our younger generations missed out on some of the experiences that we had, but then we wouldn't want anyone to have to go through what our folks went through, would we?

Gladys McDonald, who grew up in Mortlach, Saskatchewan, feels that her family ate very well during the hard times of the depression.

I even surprise myself when I have difficulty remembering hard times. I guess we lived from day to day like everyone else of that era, not knowing that there were others in this world who were, supposedly, better off than we were.

I can't ever remember leaving the dinner table hungry. We started off each weekday with a healthy breakfast of oatmeal porridge. We looked forward to Sundays. There was a tradition in our family—my father was responsible for breakfast that day and his specialty was pancakes with homemade maple-flavoured syrup.

Like every other family I knew, we ate a lot of soups and stews. Sometimes it was rabbit stew from rabbits that my father hunted. We were never short of eggs or milk. Even in the little town of Mortlach where my seven siblings and I grew up, we were allowed to keep chickens and a milk cow. We had a garden in our back yard for vegetables and we grew our year's supply of potatoes on my uncle's farm a few miles away. During the summer and early fall, our kitchen was a canning factory for preserves for the winter months. Shelves in our cellar were the storage place for sealers of the colourful produce.

And I don't remember a supper without dessert—something that I don't feel is always necessary today. My mother was an expert at turning out delicious puddings—rice, tapioca, sago, chocolate, or the feature in restaurants today—bread pudding. On special occasions such as evenings when the minister and his wife, or one of the teachers had been invited to supper, we would have "Apple Brown Betty" or good old apple pie.

A bed-time snack was a ritual. Each of us enjoyed a sugar cookie and a glass of hot cocoa before snuggling up in bed.

These creative meals and snacks did not appear out of thin air or from the deli of the supermarket. I sometimes hear people talk about how "uneducated" women were then, especially country wives who never made it past grade school. Granted, many knew little about algebra or the Punic Wars or the Big Bang Theory. But I think anyone who had as many skills and as much wisdom as the women who kept their families fed, clothed, and sustained in Spartan conditions cannot be called uneducated. Unschooled, perhaps, but that is another matter.

Dorothy Evans of Moose Jaw, Saskatchewan, was kind enough to give me a copy of a poem her mother, Florence Jane McKague, wrote about prairie women. Mrs. McKague died in 1941.

THE WESTERN MOTHER

To waste in no way must she try,
Or leave the household budget shy.
So she never thought to shirk
A single task of all her work.

Soap she made from bacon chips,
Quilts she pieced from rag bag snips.
She ground the dried up parts of bread
For puddings: Sheets upon the bed
Were laid the wrong way up with care
(Except when company was there)
To save the hemstitched tops from wear.

The meat she canned, the chickens, too.
The vegetables did the season through.
For fruit used citron, squash, and marrow.
She cut old clothes to fit if narrow.
Shirts and aprons from flour sacks
Were worn upon her children's backs.
Paraffin from jellies clear
Was saved and used from year to year.
Made coffee out of barley browned,
When extra cash was not around.
Papers magazines and string—
Bottles, boxes, everything
That could be used again, she kept.

The floors she covered with rag mats,
Made comforters of woollen batts.
The sheep if passing near the door
Knew by her smile she wished for more.
And even yeast cakes square and yellow
Were made by her and dried till mellow.
Butter, bacon, bread, and buns
She made to feed her hungry sons.
Cheese, too, she tried with great success
And spoiled the market in the west.
The picture frames upon the wall,

The vases, flower pots, jugs, and all, were
Made of salt and other stuff
That looked like they would cost enough.
Mitts and toques were knitted new,
Sweaters, socks, and booties, too.
Vinegar was brewed in jars.
I'll tell you what, she beat the cars.

And once when all the others slept,
She rose—because the moon was bright—
And put her pantry shelves aright.
She could not bear to waste the light!

Mrs. McKague would disagree, I am sure, about how uneducated the prairie mother was.

BELL AND MARCONI WERE
PRAIRIE BOYS AT HEART

Phones were invented decades before the thirties, radio years before, and television was then just a baby somewhere in England. It takes a while for inventions like those to become commonplace and plentiful. On the prairies, telephone poles marked the road to little towns and farms not long after the land was settled. Television was considered only a bit more impossible than space travel, but phones were in nearly every home by the thirties.

In those days, phones were connected to a "central" office in the nearest town. As many as five or six homes were on the same "line." This meant that a phone call made to one house could be heard by people living nearby who were on the same line. When one family was using the phone, others on the same line couldn't. They had to wait until the conversation was finished, signalled by a short turn of the ringer handle. It also meant that one of the favourite pastimes was "rubbering"—listening in on other people's conversations. To do this, one had to carefully lift the receiver, a Bakelite cone, from its perch, so that there was no telltale click, and just listen. Of course all conversation and any activity that was the least bit noisy in the rubberer's home had to cease entirely. One lady in our district kept a Big Ben alarm clock on top of the telephone. Its rhythmic tick-tock betrayed her every time she picked up the receiver. Nobody ever told her about it, but everyone knew when she was monitoring their conversation. Of course, pretty well everyone rubbered, but no one admitted to it.

Rubbering was not only a diversion; it was the way country folk kept abreast of the news. If someone were sick, or had an accident, good neighbours were quick to lend a hand: pick up mail and groceries if they went to town, drop by just in time to help with chores, or bring over a couple of loaves of fresh bread. Nobody ever admitted how they had found out, and nobody ever asked, either.

A couple of years into the depression, people found they could not afford to keep the telephone in their house. Some, like people in our district, paid their bill with chickens or by working on the line and managed to keep the phones. Other districts saw their phones impounded. Years and years later, someone would discover the hoard of confiscated telephones in an old barn or shed, the wood watersoaked and deteriorated. Many districts, though, just had the lines torn down and the connections to the central office disconnected. The actual telephone boxes were left in place. With typical ingenuity, farmers hooked wire onto insulators on the top of fence posts and closed the gap between gate posts by erecting a sort of bridge over the gateway—tall, slim poles tied to the end posts carried the wire high enough that traffic could get through. They might not get Central's help, but they could speak to each other—as long as their batteries lasted, anyway.

Avis Haug, now of Outlook, Saskatchewan, remembers:

> The "Bennett phone" was our way of communicating in those days: wires strung along the fences and even over the frozen river (the South Saskatchewan) by brother Carl.

The phrase "Bennett phone" refers to R. B. Bennett, a politician from Calgary whose derby hat, striped pants, and chubby face were often caricatured when he became the Canadian prime minister after his Conservative party won the election from Mackenzie King's Liberals in the early thirties. In political cartoons of the day, he was pictured as a "fat cat" who cared nothing about distressed people—as someone who helped grind them into poverty. Actually, he was quite a good man, with an unfortunate stiff aristocratic manner, who was caught in a worldwide net of depression and gloom that no one person could cure. He believed in a "market economy," and the markets of the world kept failing. Prairie people were put off by

What Makes the Wild West Wild

Cartoon from the cover of *The U.F.A.* (a publication of the United Farmers of Alberta and the Alberta Wheat Pool) depicting R. B. Bennett, 1931. *Glenbow Archives/ NA-3170-1*

his clothing, his mannerisms, and his reticence. As well as the Bennett phone, the Bennett buggy—a car with the motor removed and pulled by horses because no one could afford gasoline or repairs—was named in his "honour."

Phones may have connected people to their community, alerting them to news and, of course, gossip. But, especially on the prairie, where families often went for a week without seeing another face or hearing another voice, it was the radio that brought the world into the living room. Young men built crystal sets from kits and listened for hours to whistles and whirrs, trying to coax voices out of the ether. Family men spent far more than they ordinarily would have buying a Rogers or a DeForest Crossley—a magnificent piece of furniture. Some people, like my dad, got their radio second-hand. It had to be set up beside a window so that the aerial wire could be threaded out the little round holes in the storm window and attached to wires strung along the roof ridge. During the day it was only used to listen to the news, *The Happy Gang*, *Ma Perkins*, and *Pepper Young's Family*, and sometimes the noon *Farm Broadcast*. When it wasn't in use it was turned off because the specially purchased batteries, two B's and a C, had to last as long as possible. The A battery was usually a spare car battery that could be charged up when it went dead. Many farmers had rigged up a charger—a generator hooked up to a hand-carved propeller that spun merrily over a nearby shed. There was a great wail if the A battery went dead in the middle of *Little Orphan Annie* or *Lux Radio Theatre*.

I was about six, which means it was sometime in 1932, when I first saw a radio. Uncle Arvid was showing off a big black box with a slanted top to Dad and the uncles. He passed a pair of earphones around while he twiddled two Bakelite knobs as big as saucers. After a while, we cousins were called out from the bedroom that we used as a playroom. (It was the only room in the house besides the kitchen.) We were lined up, holding hands. Uncle Arvid grabbed the end hand and touched a little round silver hole in the black box. A shock thrilled through our line up, giving quite a jolt to the end kid, who started to cry. Mother and the aunts didn't think it was all that funny. To make up for his prank, Uncle Arvid asked if we kids wanted to listen on the earphones, but by that time we were having nothing to do with any of his ideas. Radio and earphones were both banished from the kitchen table and lunch was brought out.

The next radio I remember was at Uncle Garry's. It actually could be heard without earphones, and all the grown-ups

Harvey Haug vents his frustrations after listening to Adolph
Hilter on the radio. *Avis Haug*

gathered around it, entranced with music and news coming
from someplace called KOA Denver. It amazed us that sound
could be gathered out of thin air. Uncle Garry wasn't using an
external aerial—just a square network of wires about two feet
high that looked sort of like a cobweb. I guess it was the ances-
tor of rabbit ears. Anyhow, it was an unusual and intriguing
device. I just couldn't resist trying to see if any of it was moveable. It was. The music suddenly turned into squeals and
squawks, and I was in disgrace.

Avis Haug remembers the first time she listened to a radio.

Then came the radio, wonder of wonders. We listened to Adolph Hitler's ranting and the King's Christmas message, but more important to us, to *Ma Perkins* and *The Guiding Light*, to songs like "Red Sails in the Sunset," "Smoke Gets in Your Eyes," and "Throw Another Log on the Fire." They had catchy tunes and you could understand the words!

There was a radio station in Calgary that, at Christmas time, sponsored a used toy collection for those less fortunate. We gathered a boxful and sent it off. It was customary for the announcer to acknowledge and comment on the gifts, and we eagerly awaited hearing about ours. When the time came, my brother in his exuberance inadvertently touched the radio dial, throwing the station off centre. We missed the whole thing.

The loneliness and isolation the first settlers endured was giving way to a community solidarity. We young people knew the same songs, laughed at the same jokes on *Fibber McGee*, and thought we were up to date. Our parents listened to news stories out of Europe and thanked God there was an Atlantic Ocean. Our world was getting bigger, and closer, whether we liked it or not, and the phone and radio were the reasons we felt that way.

We know Marconi never made it far from the Eastern seaboard and Bell only managed to make it as far as Manitoba, but their inventions sparked the enthusiasm of our prairie boys for decades. In terms of ingenuity, these inventors must have been prairie boys at heart.

BEYOND HORSEPOWER

During the teens and the twenties of the last century, rural transportation gradually changed from hay-fed horsepower to gasoline-fed horsepower. Every family has its legends of the patriarch who, sitting reluctantly at the wheel of an automobile his sons had talked him into buying, hauled back on the steering wheel and yelled "Whoa!" as he drove it through the back wall of the garage.

By 1930 nearly every family had a car—some even had small trucks—"two chicken" trucks we would call them now. Many of the cars were Model T Fords, but there were also Chevs, Nashs, Whippets, Dodges, and Buicks—some are brand names still familiar today; others have become a part of history. Most cars were plain Jane, black and boxy, but there were notable exceptions. Uncle Arvid's dark green sedan had a trunk on the back— a real trunk, separate, square, with a lid that locked shut and leather straps to help keep it that way. Between the front and rear doors there was a little cut-glass flower vase inside on each doorpost.

As the depression of the 1930s developed, some people found they could not afford to keep their beloved cars on the road, at least not in the way they had become used to, and along came the "Bennett buggy." This was a car body with the motor removed and tongue and doubletree eveners added so it could be pulled by horses, its occupants shielded from the weather and sitting in comparative luxury compared to a "democrat" or buggy. The Bennett buggy is the definitive archetype of the depression, a make-do, a make-over, a sneer at the politicians, and a symbol of defiance as well. But not all cars were turned into Bennett buggies.

Dad's Model T was one that kept going. It was pretty basic— two doors, high and wide windows, a flat roof, hand-operated windshield wiper, a lever and three pedals on the floor in front of the driver, gas and choke levers on the steering column, a motor—and a crank. The crank, along with horror stories about backfires that destroyed the cranker's thumb or broke his wrist, was the reason why most women were the driven, not the drivers. (It surely wasn't a matter of strength. Nobody worried about a woman being strong enough to carry a couple of pails of water to the house, or to pitch hay or sheaves, or for that matter to do the family wash with exotic equipment like boilers, tubs, scrub boards, and clotheslines.)

Dad took good care of his Model T. Every weekend he took it to the dugout in Grandpa's pasture and washed it so it would look decent when we went to church. In late fall, when the roads got tough, he put it up on blocks in the garage. And in spring he put a binder canvas out on the ground to lay out all the bits and pieces when he overhauled the motor. Among his tools there was a neat wooden rod with a suction cup on top that stuck on to each valve in turn, as he ground it smooth with an emery compound. We girls thought of several interesting things we could stick that suction cup onto, but Dad wouldn't let us go near it.

We used that car right through the thirties, although toward the end, things started to wear out, especially the tires. There was no way Dad could renew them by purchase or trade so we always started for church about half an hour ahead of time. When there is no spare, it takes a while to fix a flat tire.

In one incident, we left at ten o'clock for the eleven o'clock service four miles away. Just outside our farm yard gate, the right rear tire blew. Dad got out and collected his equipment from under the driver's seat, and I crawled out the back window to help—or at least watch. Carolie and Carl were about to follow me, but Mom, who was holding baby Kay on her lap, made use of a tight lip and evil eye to change their mind. Dad jacked up the wheel, removed it, dismantled it, found the puncture in the tube, scratched around the hole with the little grater from the top of the patch box, smeared on some goo from a small tube to make the patch stick, peeled the cover off the patch, and firmly

(Left to right) Carolie, Eileen, and their mother, with Kay and Carl Jr. in front, pose in front of the Model T. *Eileen Comstock*

pressed it on. He then put the tube back in the tire, put the tire onto the wheel, the wheel onto the car, and attached the hose of the hand pump to the tube's valve. Putting one foot on a flip out loop at the bottom of the pump to anchor it, he inflated the tube with air, checking the pressure with a bullet-shaped, silver-coloured gauge. Out from under came the jack. It, the pump, the patch box, the goo, and the gauge went back under his seat. I crawled in again through the back window. Dad spun the crank, dusted off his knees, got in, and away we went, not even late for service!

Although we did use the car, our travel was never very extensive. We went to church, to Cadillac for shopping, and to Swift Current once or twice a year. Our yearly visit to Mom's sister in Rush Lake, about sixty miles away, was about the farthest we ever went.

Beth Byggdyn and her friend had a car trip as teenagers in 1934. Her memory of going from Prince Albert to Moose Jaw illustrates that such a long trip was a very big deal, indeed.

My First Trip to Moose Jaw—Early morning of July 19, 1934, found me and my school chum Wilna in the rumble seat of a little coupe car bound for our church's annual camp meeting, at that time held south of Moose Jaw in what is now Wakamow Valley. Driving the car was a Mr. R. and sharing the front seat was Wilna's aunt, a Miss B., who, when not on holidays, taught school in Prince Albert. Wilna had just turned fifteen; I would reach that milestone in August. Both of us had just completed Grade Nine. Neither of us had been farther than sixty miles from home.

Because Moose Jaw was over two hundred miles from our homes at Davis, south of Prince Albert, and because the roads then were gravelled, not paved, we started for Moose Jaw around four in the morning. The coupe couldn't travel much faster than thirty miles per hour. We took along a picnic lunch and expected to reach Moose Jaw about suppertime. There we were to go to a hotel and freshen up, as Mr. R's sister, a Mrs. Hales, owned the hotel at that time.

We travelled south on what was then (and still is) Number Two highway. The terrain was quite familiar until we came to Dana and its large lake. I had never before seen a lake covered with sodium sulphate. (Today much of that has disappeared, but then the lake bed was dry and covered with the white precipitate.) As we proceeded south and left the treed area behind, I was amazed to see nothing but mile after mile of Russian thistle, stones, and endless telephone poles stretching into the distance; nothing green or growing, until we reached the Qu'Appelle Valley and stopped on the bank of a small stream where green plants were growing. Those hills resembled what I thought little mountains might look like. (I had never seen mountains, either.)

Before reaching the Qu'Appelle, we had stopped at Simpson for our travel break and ate our picnic lunch. By that time Wilna and I looked like Negroes. We had put cold cream on our faces to protect us from the sun, and the dust, finding a great place to stick, had blackened our faces.

We reached Moose Jaw about six o'clock, cleaned up, then drove out to the camp. I recall seeing the giant picture of Robin Hood on the wall of the mill as we crossed the Fourth Avenue bridge. When we reached camp, our tents had to be set up, mattresses filled with straw and then we lined up for supper in the dining hall. The line of more than two hundred people stretched for quite a way from the door of the dining hall. Our meal tickets only cost $1 each for the ten days, I suppose because most of the food was donated, and all the work done by volunteers. Wilna's aunt gave us girls the meal tickets as even $1 was too much for our parents to afford in those days.

That night, seated for services in the large tent that served as the camp auditorium, I watched the wind blow the tent walls in and out. I fancied that I could see the miles of desert-like terrain, complete with stones, on the billowing walls of the tent. Next morning, rested, I was ready to enjoy camp activities, meet new people, and make new friends.

I mentioned that women didn't usually drive back then—well, my mother learned to drive. Barely. She hesitated shifting from high gear to low on one of her first solo trips, so she powered out going up the steep hill just north of our gate. The motor quit. The Model T started to go backwards down the hill. It came to a stop at the bottom, in the middle of the road, between two sharp ditches. Mom hadn't jumped and run. She had steered it to safety. But when the emergency was over she got out of the car, walked home, and as far as I know that was the end of her driving career. She exclaimed, "Maybe I can't drive, but I am a great steerer!"

Avis Haug of Outlook, Saskatchewan, tells about the beginning and end of her driving career.

It so happened that on one occasion I was recruited to drive the truck home from the field where Harvey was on the tractor. I did, in low gear all the way! When I stepped out I was shaking so that my legs would hardly support me, so that was the end of any driving for me. Many, many years later, I toyed with the idea of driving lessons, and dreamt of owning a Karman Ghia, only to hear of a woman student driver who stepped on the gas instead of the brakes and ended up drowned in the nearby river. I lost interest, immediately and permanently.

Toward the middle of the thirties our car started to show its age. The Model T had bands that were engaged when it was put into gear. With age the bands for the forward gears loosened and tended to slip under load. Reverse bands never got much use and remained strong. Now, going to Swift Current, forty-seven miles away, was an occasion for our family. Grandma Kopperud often came along and took her accustomed place, between us sisters in the middle of the back seat. Dad drove. Mother sat in the "mamma's" seat holding Baby Carl in her lap. We always started early, as at twenty miles an hour it took the best part of the morning to get there.

And almost always, about four miles south of Swift Current, where the gravel highway curved its way uphill to the northwest from a wide valley to the top of the row of hills, we had problems. The Model T would slow down, shudder its way into low gear, and soon the motor was racing away but the wheels weren't going around. Dad always knew what was about to happen, and by the time we stopped moving he would already have pulled off to the side of the road. We passengers exited and started the long walk to the top of the hill. Dad got the car turned around and after a little while he would come puttering past our pedestrian caravan, driving in reverse. At the top of the hill, he turned the car's nose toward Swift Current and we piled back in.

Our old car certainly had its faults and problems but it served us well. It got us where we were going and home again, and after all, isn't that what a vehicle is supposed to do?

How to Celebrate Christmas

When I was little, Christmas week was the time when our extended family sort of went overboard in the visiting department. By the time Grandma, Mom, and about five aunts had each played hostess to the entire group, the week was pretty well over. The dinner menus always included things peculiar to a Scandinavian Christmas, such as lutefisk and lefse. As well, each lady had her specialty. Aunt Clara always served what she called "Waldorf Salad"—a blend of sliced apples, bananas, and crushed walnuts, all smothered in thick whipped cream with red maraschino cherries spread judiciously across the top. Aunt Mina's forte was a corn soufflé, puffy and cheesy. Heaven help anybody who wasn't ready to eat the minute that came out of the oven. Mom's mincemeat pie and carrot pudding were her specialties, although I had to grow up before I learned to appreciate mincemeat anything!

The afternoon of December 24th seemed to last forever. I am sure we kids were ready to leave for Grandpa's house hours before Mom and Dad started to get ready. Mom had baby paraphernalia to get ready, gifts to round up and pack, herself and Baby Carl to get ready, as well as having to check us older ones to make sure we hadn't gone overboard in our zeal to look good. Dad did chores up early and finished them off by setting a sheaf of grain upright on a post by the barn: Christmas for the birds. After changing out of his chore clothes, he brought the team and cutter to the door. We set off on the half-mile jaunt to Grandpa's across the snow-covered pasture. I am sure the weather didn't always cooperate and that things were not all sweetness and light, but in my memory that trip was always serene—a star-studded sky above us and white snow all around us. The only sounds were the breathing of the horses, the tinkle of harness, and the swish of sleigh runners through the snow.

After the commotion of getting everybody's overshoes lined up behind the stove, and coats, hoods, scarves, and mittens tossed on the big bed in the bedroom, Carolie and I and our cousins got out from under the grown-ups' eyes and found our own brand of fun, reasonably quiet so that we didn't attract any notice that might bring a bellow in our direction. We had lots of time because the grown-ups always got to eat at the first table setting and they seemed to take forever downing their share of lutefisk dowsed with melted butter, meatballs and gravy, creamed peas and carrots, mashed potatoes, pickles, lefse, buns, and dessert. And then they always had to finish off with "just a half cup more coffee, thanks."

After a bit of dishwashing and table resetting, we kids and the leftover grown-ups ate our fill. Soon everybody ended up around the piano in the living room, singing carols, both English ones that even we kids knew by heart and old Norwegian ones from the slim black choirbooks called the *Fridetoners*. The harmony was great, and after a while the volume became even a bit overwhelming. Our family loved to sing.

Later one of the aunts quieted everybody down to listen while the youngest reader worked his or her way through the Christmas story from Luke, with the audience silently mouthing hard parts like "Cyrenius, the governor of Syria," in encourage-ment. Then Grandma brought out a plate of Japanese oranges and bowlsful of candy and nuts still in their shells. All that singing must have settled everybody's big supper because soon we were all munching again. There was competition among the grown-ups for possession of the two nut-crackers, while in a quiet corner Grandpa took out his well-worn pocket knife, deftly peeled Brazil nuts out whole, and gave most of them to us kids.

In a while there was a commotion in the verandah and in came Santa Claus. Our Santa didn't wear a red suit—in fact he wore an old fur coat that sort of looked like the one Grandpa wore when he drove the team to town on bitterly cold days. His face was pretty well hidden under a toque and scarf. He did a lot of foolish things, like chasing the aunts and kissing them and mussing our hair, calling the three rolls of curls on top of our heads "culverts." We knew it was one of the uncles, but in the excitement of the hour we always forgot to see which one was missing. Santa finally settled down, distributed the gifts, and left through the verandah again, yelling at his reindeer as he went.

The gifts were opened, and everybody had to look at everybody else's before it was time to leave. Mothers gathered their family's gear into the big boxes they had come with, got everybody back into coats and overshoes again, and a much more sombre bunch travelled home. Next day after church service, we would all be together again for another feast, an afternoon of playing in the snow or trying to win playing "pick-up-sticks" or "Flinch" with the grown-ups at the dining room table. It was starting to be a wonderful week to be a kid!

Beth Byggdyn's Christmas, near Prince Albert, Saskatchewan, was also a "Grandma" celebration, with a difference.

She wasn't really my grandma. My maternal grandmother died before I was four so my memory of her is faint; my paternal grandma I never saw, for she lived in Hespeler, Ontario, and all I knew of her was a faded snapshot and occasional cards, letters or gifts at Christmas. I am sure she loved us but we were far away and she had many Ontario grandchildren near by. Grandma Breeden was really the grandmother of my school chum. She lived only a mile or so from our farm home, and she and her husband opened their hearts and home to take in our family, with theirs, for several Christmases during the thirties.

Christmas morning, breakfast cleared away and chores done, we—Dad, Mother, two brothers, and four sisters— dressed in our best, sped across the snowy fields behind Maud and Nellie (or Lucy and Lady), one of Dad's two teams of drivers, to the Breeden home. There, the team was made comfortable in the barn while we entered a house redolent with delicious aromas, removed our coats, and found seats in the living room until called to dinner by "Auntie Beulah," the adult, unmarried Breeden daughter largely responsible for putting Christmas dinner on the table.

That table was something to see! At each place was a Japanese orange with one of our names on it. In the centre of the table was a dish of butter "carved" to look like a pineapple, little dishes of candy and nuts interspersed with salads and cranberry sauce, and, just before dinner was called, hot vegetables, a bowl of dressing and the turkey or sometimes a goose, which was browned to perfection before being sliced and set down in front of Grandpa Breeden. We found our places from the orange "placecards" and ate until we could eat no more. Desserts included Christmas pudding with sauce, mince pies, even ice cream, homemade and delicious.

Dinner over, we visited with the Breeden grandchildren—some of them our age—or around four o'clock rode with Grandpa Breeden behind his team of drivers, the mile or so to Davis station, to meet his daughter and two children coming from Prince Albert to join the crowd at the farm for the remainder of the Christmas celebration.

By the time we were back at the house it would be suppertime. Fresh buns, cold turkey, salads, followed by beautifully iced cakes, cookies, fruit cake, dainties, and ice cream, plus hot beverages for adults and milk or cocoa for the children, made us replete.

The Breedens had a large mantel radio, complete with a gramophone-shaped speaker. After supper, if King George V was scheduled to speak, we gathered in the living room, straining to hear every word. After that, dishes done, we sat in a large circle and played games: "Poor Pussy," "I've a Bright Idea," and the like. By the time of the last Christmases at the Breeden home, both their older grandchildren and their two youngest daughters had boyfriends who joined the group. One of these was "Jay" who later married Beulah. I recall, while playing "Poor Pussy," Jay could make the most horrific "meows" without cracking a smile, but the person who had to pat his head could rarely keep from laughing, so that person then had to be the Poor Pussy. My little brother, Everett, then in the primary grades, gave us a laugh when playing "How Does It Resemble Me?" The item chosen was the wick of a coal oil lamp in the room. When asked how it resembled him, Everett said, "Sometimes it needs a little trimming." "Trimming" was my father's term for the switch or strap, but Father laughed as heartily as anybody at that one.

About ten o'clock, at the latest, we would say our thanks for another lovely Christmas Day at the Breeden home and, nestled under blankets in the sleigh box, speed across the fields to home. There the fire was rekindled to warm the house before we went to bed and while the house warmed we'd enjoy the last hour of another Christmas day.

Wallace Byggdyn's Christmas memories sound a little more strenuous than Beth's.

Christmas at Uncle Henry's and Aunt Hilda's home, across the Qu'Appelle Valley, was always special. Their two boys and one girl were slightly younger than we but not too young to be playmates. Christmas forenoon we would travel in our horse-drawn, covered sleigh, for one and a half hours. I remember their Christmas tree was lit by real candles, fastened to the branches with little clips. They looked very pretty but weren't allowed to burn long, in case of fire. After admiring the tree we sat down to Aunt Hilda's delicious Christmas dinner with all the trimmings. It may have been the dirty thirties, but Uncle Henry was pretty well fixed for those days and he—a Norwegian— and his Swedish wife spread a good table, especially at Christmas.

One Christmas afternoon our cousins and we used a bobsleigh to give us all a ride down a valley hill. One boy stood on the sleigh and steered the bobsleigh by pushing on the tongue. The hard part was getting that heavy sleigh up the hill again. We had to push it up, and those Qu'Appelle Valley hills are not small!

Avis Haug's Christmas memories involve the extended family that lived in the same area, near Ardath, Saskatchewan.

In retrospect, I suppose one's earliest memories are those of Christmases. It was practically the "law of the Medes and Persians" that we alternate Christmas and New Year's dinners with my aunt and uncle, who lived a mile or so north of us. We lugged our gifts along to show off and play with. It was standing tradition when I was old enough that I receive the next book or two in the Elsie Dinsmore series. One particular year that stands out in memory was when on our way for Christmas dinner, our sleigh box overturned. (When we got back to school we had to write a story about our holiday. I entitled mine "An Upside Down Sleigh Ride on Christmas Day" and was rewarded with a "Very Good" mark.)

But Christmas Eve was even more special. The house had to be cleaned upstairs and down, and no decorating was done until it was. Dad and brother Harvey did the outside chores while Mom and I did up the dishes after the traditional lutefisk supper. The chores seemed to take longer than usual and no wonder. The animals each had to have an extra portion and an oat sheaf had to be put out for the birds. The climax of the evening came when one of my brothers played Santa Claus and doled out the gifts. In later years I remember there being a program. My youngest brother, Ted, was into "Sunday School at Home" at that time, and at the end of the program, he took up an offering—about 80 cents—and sent it to the Sunday School at Home.

Christmas concerts were the highlight of the winter for rural districts. We began practising early in the fall, and how is it we could memorize pages and pages and pages then, while now we struggle with one single Bible verse? Then Christmases seemed years apart, and now we barely put the decorations away before it is time to take them out again.

And what would Christmas be without the Christmas concert? These concerts were the highlight of the year for many children of the thirties. At these events every child was a star! In the little white school houses, the rural schools on the prairie, the Christmas concert was just about the most important event in a school kid's life, at least from the beginning of November on. And it was just about the most important event in a schoolteacher's life, too. It was rural consensus that a "good" teacher put on a good concert, and as a former rural schoolteacher, I know that a good part of a teacher's reputation was built on the success of the concert. Not that I minded. I enjoyed being in concerts when I was in school, and I thoroughly enjoyed putting them on.

There were only half a dozen "play books" that contained humorous skits, and they were part of every teacher's ammunition. Once it had been established which "plays" had been used the previous couple of years so as to avoid repetition, a teacher would choose several plays to do for the coming concert. Choice depended on how many actors were required, how many pupils were available, and how elaborate the props had to be. The parts for each actor were copied out by the bigger kids. Other concert standbys were a humorous drill for the boys, a cute drill for the girls, recitations, carol singing, and of course, the Pageant, usually a Nativity scene. I always tried to make sure each child had at least two speaking parts. Sometimes it was only saying a line in an acrostic while holding a coloured cardboard letter in a line up that spelled "Christmas" or "Greetings" and a short recitation, if the child was little and shy, but it was amazing how easily children learned complicated lines and really got into acting.

One of my most embarrassing moments came about three days before the concert in my first school, when all the pupils' desks were bunched on one side of the room. The stage took up a good part of the front by the blackboards, and some of the kids were up there going through one of the skits. Others were at their desks finishing up some arithmetic, and I was jumping from one thing to another as needed. All of a sudden Mr. Fraser, my school superintendent, walked into the room. Oh, he had been there before, but that time I had everything under control, lesson plans all laid out, all the kids cooperating by behaving themselves, and I considered that I had put on a pretty good demonstration of "how a teacher should keep school." This seemed to me to be utter chaos. I can't tell you how relieved I was when he didn't stay long. (And I was both surprised *and* relieved when I got a copy of his report to the trustees, saying all sorts of nice things about how well things were going at the school.)

We made a crepe paper backdrop for the Nativity scene, green fields, dark blue sky, Bethlehem on the horizon, and a gold star on high. One of the families brought a pump organ the day of the concert, so I played backup music for our carols. On stage were the shepherds in their parents' bathrobes with striped towels tied with black cord for headgear; the angels folded into white sheets with tinsel in their hair; three kings in robes and gold paper crowns, carrying glittering gifts; serious Joseph standing behind Mary, who wore a pale blue gown and white head square and knelt holding the swaddled Baby in her arms; and to cap it all—the two little Grade One sheep with long white drawers pulled on over their clothes, perky ears perched on their heads, and curly tails pinned behind. The audience of mothers and fathers, aunts and uncles, and the neighbours were quiet and attentive. My children sang like angels, better than I had ever heard them before. There were tears in my eyes and a lump in my throat. I asked the audience to help us sing the final carol, "Silent Night." It was beautiful.

Madge Bennett, who grew up near Wapella, Saskatchewan, taught in both the south of the province where native trees were scarce and further north, where the landscape was very different. It even made a difference to the Christmas concert.

Another school I taught at was in northern Saskatchewan. There were many Doukhobor and Ukrainian families in my new district, and the people were very friendly. There were a lot of trees. I grew up in the "bluff" area in southern Saskatchewan and was not accustomed to seeing native evergreens growing on their own in what were also called bluffs—very different from the bushy little clusters I had known. Of course, every year at Christmas time, there had to be a school Christmas concert. The children were busy for the last month preparing and memorizing their parts and the songs. In this more northern area snow generally came earlier in the fall than it did further south on the prairie, so most of the children came to school by cutter or sleigh. On the day before the concert when it was time to decorate and prepare the school for the big event, several of the older boys took a team and sleigh and went to a nearby creek to cut down a Christmas tree. To my surprise, they came back with a lovely big evergreen for us to trim and a couple of smaller trees. We cut the smaller ones apart and used the branches for greenery to put over the doors and windows. As well as the beauty of the foliage, there was a lovely pine tree aroma to greet everyone who came for the evening's entertainment.

So many of the memories the "children of the thirties" shared with me for this book have to do with memorable meals—especially Christmas meals—that it sounds as if hunger was not a problem. For many it wasn't. For some it was harsh reality. Especially for one group—the men who took to the road, who rode the rods. Many of these were still almost boys who, when they realized there was no way of making a living in the district they had grown up in, decided to look elsewhere for work. If by leaving, there would be a little more at home for the rest of the family to share, all the better. Surely, a man who was willing to work would be able to support himself. It was a futile dream.

So many had the same despair or the same vision that soon the hundreds and then thousands of them became seen by the authorities not as men looking for work but as vagrants, tramps, or hoboes. Many municipalities, already stressed by having to provide assistance to needy residents, passed by-laws to the effect that if a stranger asked for help, municipal agents were allowed to give him one meal, on condition that he leave the district immediately.

Federal and provincial governments felt threatened so they adopted harsh methods. Work camps—virtual prison camps—were established far from populated areas, and men were herded into them. They were given enough food to keep them alive, sometimes a wage of a few cents a day, and provided with work. Often it was "make work," such as one day piling up wood and the next day unpiling it. Camps provided fertile soil for trouble to grow. Even Communist propaganda started sounding like a sensible alternative to their present situation.

The work camps spawned the "Trek to Ottawa" march of the unemployed, the homeless, the dispossessed; the trek ended tragically in what was called the "Regina Riot." It is sad to realize that toward the end of the thirties though better weather improved prospects for crops on the farm, it took World War II to improve economics. Many of the unemployed enlisted in the armed forces, perhaps to kill or to be killed, and most of the rest found work in war-related industry. I find it peculiar that money can be found for war, but not to relieve desperation.

Joseph Payjack, Jr., lives, as his family has for decades, in Winnipeg, Manitoba. His story of true generosity offered to a down-and-out young man who was riding the rails during the hard times reminds of why so many people have retained some positive memories of the Great Depression.

Although I am now in my seventies I was too young to recall this experience on my own. You know how kids are swept up by the excitement of Christmas. However, my mother, four older sisters and a brother, as well as other family members, confirm this story.

We lived on Higgins Avenue in an area of Winnipeg still known as Point Douglas. Higgins is an avenue running east and west on the south side of, and parallel to, the CPR main line. Our house was about three blocks east of the CPR depot and the now long-gone CPR Royal Alexander Hotel. Point Douglas was a decent but far from affluent neighbourhood, at that time feeling the effects of the Great Depression.

For those men riding the rails during the depression, Christmas must have been a low point. But individual acts of charity toward these destitute men were not uncommon. *Glenbow Archives/NC-6-12955B*

On Christmas day, 1931, we were preparing to have our dinner. Our family, also harshly affected by the times, somehow was still able to lay out a truly festive table—turkey, root-cellar vegetables, preserves, and traditional Ukrainian fare. The house was full. Not only our immediate family but uncles, aunts, and cousins were there to make it a true family affair.

There was a knock at the door, and my father answered. A young boy, perhaps eighteen years old or so, stood before my dad and asked for a bite to eat or a few cents. Without hesitation, my dad asked the boy in and immediately made him feel comfortable and at ease. He had a way of making people feel welcome, and so I have learned, was generous to a fault.

Dad proceeded to help the boy clean up, for he had just gotten off the freight train. He had been "riding the rods" as it was termed—a common occurrence in those days. The young man was given a clean shirt, and, a short time later, our guest came downstairs to join our family for dinner. He spent the night on the chesterfield and in the morning, after breakfast, my dad rounded up some spare warm clothing, packed a lunch with Christmas leftovers and, I was told, also gave him an undisclosed amount of cash.

Three and a half years later, on June 24, 1935, my father passed away from pleurisy. He was thirty-eight years old. This I remember well. He was well-known and well-liked, and needless to say it was a large funeral.

One day a few years later, my mother answered a knock at the door. The man facing her smiled and said hello. Mom thought he looked a bit familiar but couldn't place him. He asked if he could see Mr. Payjack. When Mother told him of my dad's passing, the man broke down and wept openly. Regaining his composure, he told my mother that the gesture of kindness displayed that Christmas in 1931 not only helped save his life, but it was a "stepping stone" to a new beginning. He offered my mother a sum of money, but she would not accept it, even though she probably could have used it. She just said, "That is the way my husband would want it to be." The young man left and we never heard from him again.

Saving Up to Get Married

Many young men had to leave their home area to find work during the depression. A young farmhand-cum-cowboy named Bert Kitchen, from Wainwright, Alberta, was one of them. He was trying to make enough money so that he could afford to marry his sweetheart. Bert and some of his brothers headed to Jasper, Alberta, to try their luck. Below are excerpts from letters he sent to his fiancée, Melba Plaxton, that tell a story of grit and perseverance.

Feb. 20, 1930: Arrived in Jasper on the train. Stopped off in Edmonton to talk to Newt Babb.

Feb. 22: (Letterhead reads "National Hotel, JC Forsythe, Manager) Job hunting, weather warm, thawing daily, mountains beautiful.

Feb. 25: (Letterhead reads "Hughes and Kitchen, Guides and Outfitters, Jasper Park, Alberta) No work yet. Has Marvin heard anything about the well yet?

Mar. 6: Working at the lodge. Transportation "two bits" a day to ride out in their truck.

Mar. 11: Working at the lodge, sometimes with pick and shovel, sometimes on cement mixer. They canned about thirty men today, but I am still working. Three hundred men working at the lodge and expect that they will hire about another hundred.

Mar. 17: Could work all summer … don't think that there will be any crop this year as the ground is so dry now that it would have to rain for a month before it would even get damp. The others have gone to a big masquerade dance. They all wanted me to go, but I told them that I would if my girl was here. Jim told me that I could have the loan of his once in a while. I told him "thank you— the one I have is enough for me."

Mar. 19: Bad storm ... no work today. Got a letter from Newt at Edmonton saying that he is broke and trying to sell life insurance but not selling very much. How many of the boys have come back from Turner Valley?

Apr. 6: Lonesome Sunday ... walked fifteen miles and took three rolls of pictures. Still working and had better stay with it until I hear of something down there.

Apr. 10: Jack back after a visit to Wainwright—reporting that there are sure a lot of men out of work down there.

Apr. 17: I get so darned lonesome for you that I don't know what to do with myself. I guess that I can get a job with Brewster if I want—guiding over at the lodge. Not enough money as they only pay about $80 a month. If I had my car up here I could make a few dollars a day running taxi in the evenings.

Apr. 21: Just got back from a car ride about forty miles down the highway with brother Stanley trying to find some of his horses—darned near froze driving in an open Ford car. Saw about one hundred wild sheep. Going to write Marvin a letter tonight. Ain't quite sure when I will start for home but hope it will be soon—will have to come back here for the summer as I don't think there will be any work down Wainwright way. Going to be a lot of roadwork done here this summer. Hope you have a good time at the dance at Rosedale.

Apr. 22: I expect to come back about a week from next Sunday. I may get that packing job for the government, so you see, sweetheart, it will pay your old man to stick around for a while. Of course I can get a good job here in the fall as Stanley has got four different parties to take out hunting this fall and I guess that I will be taking one of them.

May 1: (Bert in Wainwright for a few days)

May 18: Drove back to Jasper with Tom. Got into Jasper at half-past six—only had two punctures. Lots of mud when leaving Edmonton. May get job with the government in a couple of days—$6 a day—guiding out on the trail.

May 20: Haven't started to work yet. Very quiet—about forty men laid off at the lodge.

May 27: Got a job for 50 cents an hour and only nine hours a day working on the Jasper Park stampede grounds. It will only last for about three weeks.

June 3: Received the pictures ... still working for the Horseman's Assoc. building corrals and three miles of fence. Got Tommy O'Riley a job about forty miles out of town driving team on the government road up to the Hot Springs.

June 5: Just received a letter from Edmonton from a man that wants me to go up to Fort Smith and run a well drilling outfit for him ... I expect to get about $10 a day and all expenses and it will last til next fall. If I take the job I will drive down to Wainwright before I go up there. Then there will be wedding bells this fall. I could not spend any money up there ... all my expenses paid, but I guess that I would have to buy my own stuff.

June 6: Last night drove a couple of men over to the lodge and made $1.50, and then took four people down to Pokahontas and made $11 and my gas bill.

June 8: Sunday ... Have been working all day and have just had supper and now going down to Pokahontas. Take a load of boys down and bring up a load of boys ... make about $10. Last night had bad luck ... broke the battery out of the car. Hit a rock that flew up and knocked the outside right off it.

June 10: Got a new job for a few days riding for a moving picture outfit, the Fox Films Movie Zone outfit ... $7.50 a day. Oh yes, sweetheart, I am one of the Royal Northwest Mounted Police when I am riding for their movie so I guess that you will be seeing your old man on the screen some day ... I will find out what the picture is called.

June 15: My dearest darling, I am out at Brewster Camp tonight and this is the first chance that I have had to write. It is now about twelve o'clock. I am out packing and riding for the moving picture outfit and expect to be with them for about three weeks. Have been working a long day today, made about $12. Don't expect to make quite as big a haul from now on as we won't get in as long days. We are on our way to Medicine Lake tomorrow and have to pack all the machinery for the picture outfit on horseback from there to wherever they want to go.

June 18: (Letterhead reads "Brewster's Rocky Mountain Camps, Jasper Park) It is snowing here to beat the band. There are about eight inches of snow here. The whole of the moving picture outfit are up here with us, and I don't think that they like it very well ... I have smashed the end of my little finger and it sure is sore. We have packed all the moving picture stuff up here ... it just took us two days with forty pack horses each day. We sure had some trip as my outfit was half of them broncs and I sure did have some fun getting my packs on the first time but I have got them broke now so I can get close enough to put the packs on them. For ever ...

June 19: We all have got steady jobs up here at $5 a day, and when we ride for the movies we get $10 a day. I helped to pack about thirty-five horses and then we had to take them about twenty-four miles and it rained all the time that we were on the trail. We have only three girls here and one maid for the star actress. They sure are one wild bunch so I don't bother with them at all. Sure have had some bad weather. It has either rained or snowed every day, and these movie people are just about fed up with it.

June 24: Well, Melba dear, here I am back in Jasper again. The weather was so bad that the moving picture men had to call it all off. But I am working as usual. I am back helping to fix up the stampede grounds. I sure would like to drop down and spend the first of July with my sweetheart, but I guess that I can't afford the trip just yet. I expect there will be lots of work here in a week as the tourists are starting to come in.

Say, sweetheart, I was one of the main actors in the picture here. I had to ride out in the rapids on Maligne River and rope one of the boys that got upset in a canoe, and I sure did a good job of it. I caught him on the first throw with my rope right over his neck, and he was so close to being dead that I had to haul him out with my horse and lift him up on the saddle and pack him into camp. They all say that I was the hero of the day, and all I got for it was $20. But I guess I would have done my best to save the guy's life if I didn't get anything for it. I am feeling kind of blue tonight ... no place to go and nobody to hug but I guess that everything will come out all right after a while.

June 27: Received your short note and am still waiting for a letter. Still working at the stampede grounds. There is going to be a stampede here on the first of July, and if I have not got a job by then I will have to try to do a little riding. Guess I will be all right by then, I mean my finger. I have smashed it just between the nail and the first joint, but it is feeling quite a bit better and I can bend it a little but it sure is some size yet. I am sending you a couple of pictures of your new policeman. Write and tell me how you like my outfit.

What is Marvin doing? Has he finished his breaking yet and is he going to work on the oil well. Write and tell me all the news.

July 2: You asked me what I did on July 1st. Well, sweetheart, I rode in the bucking contest yesterday. They did not have enough horses to make a stampede out of it but I made about $15 and I didn't get bucked off either. I got second in the stake race and also a second in the hundred yard cowboy's race, and I received a windbreaker and a whole carton of smoking tobacco. Sunday I worked on the stampede grounds all day. I have worked every Sunday since I came up here and today is the first day that I haven't worked since I started up here and I didn't get out of bed until noon ... Made $5 today taking a party of men out for a drive.

July 6: Have got a job for a few days ... am helping a man load a few car loads of bricks ... not a very good job for my sore finger but it is coming along all right.

Bert Kitchen (with lariat) performing the "wedding ring." *Pat Humphreys*

Have washed the car and shined her all up just like new. How are the crops looking? We have showers here every day of the week and cold all the time. I don't think that we are going to have any warm weather this summer. Stanley has just come back from a fishing trip. He was getting a bunch of fish for Sir Henry Thornton. He got forty-five trout for him and twenty-seven for himself so I guess that I will have some fresh fish for dinner.

July 15: Just landed back into town from Edmonton. We all went to the fair ground and saw all there was to see. Will send you a pair of red earrings tomorrow [red was Melba's favourite colour] as I got a pair in Edmonton for you, sweetheart, and I hope that you will like them as I went to every jewellery store in the city before I could get the red ones. Tell me about your trip and also about the picnic.

July 17: Expect to get a job tomorrow. Will be going out on the trail about Saturday and will be away for five or six days on the first trip and maybe more as they may not want to come back to town. I do not know what kind of party I am going to take out but will let you know.

July 18: I am starting out on the trail in the morning and will be gone for five days on the first trip. There are three of us men taking out a party of five schoolteachers, and they are all old girls about forty years old. I leave town in the morning at nine o'clock, but the party will not leave till Sunday morning as they will go out with a car to the end of the road but we have to take the horses out to be ready for them. It looks as if it will rain for another week, but I sure hope that it will stop while I am out on this trip.

July 23: Well, sweetheart, I just caught a ride to town tonight. We are camped about eighteen miles out with the five girls, but I just had to come to town to get my letters. These five old hens that we have out are just a bunch of old maids that work in Edmonton. They are not schoolteachers at all. I will have to go now as the car is waiting to take me back.

Aug. 11: I am just getting ready to start on my trip. I am leaving Jasper tonight. This will be a short letter, sweetheart, as it is half past five and I have got to pack four horses and travel eighteen miles tonight yet, so I will have to get started soon. I have been shoeing horses for the last two days. I have not had a chew of snuff for eight days, but it sure is hard to go without it. I just feel like hell all the time but I am going to try and get along without it, but I sure do smoke a lot. Don't know for sure just when I will be going out on the trail again but expect to start about next Tuesday on a hunting trip.

Aug. 24: I have been very busy all day yesterday and today. I made $17—touring trips with the car. I am leaving town on Tuesday morning but Stan is coming down with the dudes on Wednesday evening so he can bring my mail down. I am going out for at least twenty days. There are about ten people here all talking, and I just can't seem to write a thing, dearie, I will do some talking when I get back to Wainwright.

Aug. 27: Well, sweetheart, I have started out on the hunting trip. I have been working about sixteen hours a day for the last five days getting the outfit ready to go. I will be out for about twenty-two days on this trip. I am making six dollars a day clear on this job. I have paid up my car, all but $65 and I will pay that just as soon as I get back into town again.

We are camped here at a small place called Dovoner tonight. Our dudes will not be here till tomorrow so I thought I had better write you. I don't know how I am going to post this letter but I will some way, if I have to walk all the way to Jasper. Say, brown eyes, there will be ten people altogether in our party and they are all men. One cook, one horse wrangler, and four guides, and of course there will be four dude hunters. Each one of the four guides will take a hunter out and try to show him some game to shoot at.

Sept. 19: I am going to drive a team for a week or so down at Pokahontas but may quit that any day as I have got a broken rib and if it bothers me very much I will quit and come back to town. Just a short letter, darling, as I have got to drive about thirty miles before I get to the place where I will be working and I want to get there before dark. We sure didn't have good luck on the hunting trip. The man I was guiding got five head of game, one moose, one caribou, one goat, one deer, and also a mountain sheep, so I guess that he thinks that I was a pretty good guide. He was the only man out that got five different heads to take back with him.

Sept. 21: I have not received any more mail since I came in from the hunting trip so you had better get busy and write a few letters this week. I am still driving a team down on the highway but expect to quit and take a thirty day trip. Have you had the threshers yet and if not, when do you expect them? I sure would like to be there to help you out about that time but I think that I had better stay awhile as long as I can make a little more money as I think that we will need all that I can get a hold of. If I get this trip for thirty days I will make about $200 out of it.

Oct. 2: I am working on the government roads, and I can work here until freeze up. I am driving a team but only making about $3.50 a day. I am working about thirty-eight miles from town but expect that I will be able to get in some time Saturday night. So you see that I don't have very much time to spend in town on Saturday and Sunday. I have a bath and read my mail, if there is any, and look for a job for the winter. I am sitting in my bunk writing this letter. I hope you can read it. I can hardly see to write.

Oct. 5: I received both of your letters and was sure glad to get them. I am still working on the highway but we are having quite a bit of bad weather lately so I don't know just how long it will last. The ground is so wet that they would not be able to do any roadwork. Are you still getting lots of rain or does the sun shine once in a while? Have they started to thresh again or is it too wet? Here it is raining just about as hard as it can right now and I have got to drive about thirty miles yet. I guess that the road will be pretty bad so I will have to be starting as soon as I finish writing this.

Oct. 8: I have only worked one day this week. It has been snowing here heavy since Monday night. There are eight inches of snow here. Sure is the bunk staying down here when you can't work.

Oct. 12: Well, sweetheart, here I am again. I only got in three days work last week because of the snow, and I don't think that the job will last any more than two weeks. The roads are all frozen up here today and it is cold as the devil but we are going to haul some bridge timber to build a bridge up at the end of the road. Soon as we get the timber hauled we will be able to roll up our bed rolls and drag out for town. For me, it will be drag to Wainwright as fast as I can go.

Oct. 19: The weather is still cold up here and I have not got another job yet, but if I don't get one pretty soon I am coming down. The roads are too bad to drive the car so I guess that I will have to take the train. I am going over to the lodge tomorrow to see about a job for the winter. I have been sitting around the shack all by myself today thinking about you.

Bert and Melba were married before the year was out—a union that lasted the rest of their lives. Melba later wrote about the depression years in the Wainwright local history book, *Buffalo Trails and Tails*.

Bert and I lived a short time in Jasper, then we went to Peace River where Bert worked the summer with a large construction crew, building the highway between Grand Prairie across the little Smokey River. As it was surveyed ahead, Bert had a caterpillar and ploughed the first furrow through. It was a life-time experience that summer. Then in the fall when the work was finished, I just couldn't wait to get back to the farm. Guess I took after my father, every little bit of me was a farmer, so we came back to go farming. With the motto, "Build your house beside the road, and be a friend to all," we rented Mr. Prior's farm for a short while. Bert rode again that winter in the Park when the bison were being rounded up. In the spring we moved onto Bert's father's farm—the original Kitchen homestead. There we spent the happiest days of our lives. I stayed at home and held the fort while every winter Bert rode in the round-ups in the park until 1939. Bert was home during the weekends. As we started farming in the hungry thirties, because of the dried-out crops the money always came in handy. The rider with two saddle horses only cleared $4.10 a day.

Anyway, we loved it all—milking cows, churning butter, getting 15 cents for a pound of butter. All you would get for your eggs was 4 or 5 cents a dozen. You would take your eggs and butter to town and trade them in on your groceries. Gee, it seemed like we had a good living on this amount. Did your washing on the scrub-board, everyone had to do that, so everybody was in the same canoe. What good times we had, dances at the school houses, picnics, etc. In those days you never dreamt of leaving your children at home. Where you went they did, too. (With permission from Melba's daughter, Pat Humphreys, Wainwright, Alberta)

RAYS OF SUNSHINE HERE AND THERE

Some stories fit into categories, although a bit of squeezing may be necessary. Some stories are gems in their own right. Many vignettes warrant a place in this collection of "sunny" stories from the thirties. Here are some of them.

Joy Mitchell, of Mitchellton, Saskatchewan, remembers the thrill of getting her first sewing machine.

In 1936, Clarence Mitchell and I were married. We had a little girl, and when she was a year old we moved from Mitchellton to the Fink farm (which we finally bought). There was a spring between the Wenman place and us. I would pack Marilyn on my hip and walk over the hummocks to visit. Mother had a sewing machine, but she wouldn't let us touch it for fear we would spoil the setting of the tension, so I didn't learn too much from her. I got to be able to sew pretty good, and Estella sold me the machine for $5. It was great to have a sewing machine at home, and I learned to sew mostly by ripping out seams and remodeling things. It was fun.

Joy made her sewing machine a "ray of sunshine" that lasted for her entire life. She made clothing, costumes, and quilts for her family and taught several 4-H classes in sewing and won prizes at fairs. Now, at eighty-three, she is a member of the Moose Jaw quilting club and still going strong.

Dorothy Gessell, of Strasbourg, Saskatchewan, remembers the quilting sessions in her mother's home, and the surrounding hijinks.

Our mother had pieced many quilts to keep us warm in bed. She used scraps left over from various sewing projects. My mother's skill on the old treadle machine kept me, her mother, and herself in clothing. However, she did not believe in using the machine to do the quilt piecing. Her even, neat hand-stitching was a delight to behold.

During our growing-up years Mother developed the habit of putting a quilt top on the frames for New Year's Day. Our living room was quite large, and the quilt occupied the middle of the room. Grandmother and Aunt and Mother would sit hunched over, diligently applying their needles. Some of the patterns were very intricate, and they took pride in their handiwork. Brother Donald and I would each thread extra needles for the quilters. We felt quite important helping the women. They would have very little left to quilt at the end of the day.

Mother had organized the food for our New Year's dinner the previous day, and Father was assigned the job of cooking it. Donald and I were to set the table. The white damask cloth that was left over from better-off days looked festive to us. (Our everyday tablecloth was the traditional oilcloth square, often well worn and cracked at the corners.)

Our grandmother was a serious "tee-totaller." She frowned upon the imbibing of any and all spirits. Father and the two brothers disappeared into the basement fairly often as the day progressed. Donald decided to see what was up. He was told to go right back upstairs. Too late! He had already seen them passing around a bottle of dandelion wine.

In order not to feel left out, Donald called me upstairs to his room. He had a precious bottle of ginger ale hidden in his clothes closet. He pinched a couple of eggcups to be our "champagne glasses." Every time the men went to the basement, the two of us would go upstairs. How special and grown-up we felt!

Harvey King was raised in the Interlake area of Manitoba between the towns of Oakpoint and Lundar. He shares his "good time" memory with us.

In 1935, my two elder sisters decided to have a double wedding. It was held in the community hall, and it was a rather quiet affair compared to today's lavish and expensive weddings. I was only eight at the time, and it was pretty exciting to me. I had just started to take an interest in dancing, and although I was clumsy, the girls didn't seem to mind. Refreshments were sandwiches and dainties served with tea and coffee. Our music came from a wind-up gramophone. (It is 1906 model, which I still own, and it still runs pretty well!)

Edith Vinge of Outlook, Saskatchewan, remembered how relieved everyone was after what could have turned out to be a tragedy turned out happily.

With the depression years came the dust storms. The dust was so thick that one could scarcely see across to the next door neighbour.

We lived in the little village of Torquay—ten miles from the United States border. To the south of our home was a mile of prairie. My sister and her friend were about six years old at the time. They loved to go to the prairie, looking for flowers and little insects. Once, while they were there, a fierce dust storm caught them. They could not find their way home so they sat down on the dried grass waiting for the storm to pass. There they sat, still huddled together when my uncle found them. There was great rejoicing when the two little girls arrived home safely.

Cecil Goddard, the man from Mitchellton, Saskachewan, who made aeroplanes, was up north at a mining camp when he witnessed an accident that could have been a tragedy but turned into a comedy.

One day I was sent to cut a piece of steel off at the base of the head frame. Bill was high up in the huge steel girders that held the head frame. He yelled down, "Hi, Cec." I looked up and saw him about thirty feet up in the 105-foot-high massive structure. I said, "Don't you fall and splash all over my new overalls." "Don't worry," he said. As I looked up at him I noticed a very heavy rope strung between two rows of girders from side to side. It was about sixty feet long, very taut and about fifteen feet high. I was about to witness the greatest miracle of my life. I heard a noise above, looked up, and saw Bill falling through the huge steel beams. There didn't seem to be a hope in the world that his head would miss the massive beams, and if they did the cement floor would smash his body to pieces. His belly hit the rope. His head and shoulders aimed straight down on one side and his legs down the other. The heavy rope stretched—he nearly touched the floor when he was jerked back up so quickly that it emptied his vest pocket onto the floor. The rope threw him off at the top, but he got a hold of it with both hands and came down safely. When his feet hit the floor, he leaned over and picked something off the floor, saying in a disgusted tone of voice, "I broke my pipe!"

Lorne Smith of Nokomis, Saskatchewan, tells about when he and his brother made a find on the way to school.

Perhaps the most vivid memory I have of the "good old days" is the time in 1930 or '31 when my brother and I were walking to school along with a teacher who boarded with our parents. On the road we found an unopened box of Copenhagen snuff. The teacher said, "You take that home to your dad (who indulged in the stuff) and do not open it at school."

Guess what? First recess one of the older chaps decided that perhaps this thing should be tapped! Everyone—just the boys of course—had a little lick. Some at noon hour and some at last recess. All went well—no problem.

After the school day was over the teacher remained to do whatever teachers did, and my brother and I proceeded home. When we got home we discovered Mother and Dad were away so we decided another pinch might be a good idea. Well the "pinches" were a bit too big. We took on a green look and the world started spinning.

Dad showed up and wondered what was the matter with us. We had to confess. I remember him reaching into his pocket and saying, "Have some more!"

I haven't had any since.

Annie Fast is a grandmother now, and known to her family as "Oma." A long time ago, when she was a teenager, she left her Mennonite family to go to the big city of Winnipeg, Manitoba, and find work. She and other girls in the same circumstance found a haven. She tells us about the "Maedchenheim."

There was no money to be made on the farm, so in 1929 my parents sent me to Winnipeg to work as a domestic. Many young girls came to the city, where they could earn from $15 to $20 a month, to help out at home. Our parents realized that being in a strange city would not be easy and that we would get homesick. When we girls came to Winnipeg, we were directed to the "Maedchenheim" or Girls Home, where we could stay until suitable work was found. The Maedchenheim was a house bought by the Mennonite community and, at the time I knew it, an elderly couple was engaged to be houseparents. The cost was 25 cents per night and 25 cents for meals. On Thursday afternoons, our half-day off, we gathered at this home to eat our lunches, which we had bought. After that a minister came to give a brief message and then we sang a lot. Someone always played the piano. We exchanged stories about our daily life, happy and sad.

This happened seventy years ago. I still remember some of the songs and still have a few friends from that time. Very few are living now.

Avis Haug, now of Outlook, Saskatchewan, reminisces about

interesting relatives whose way of life was very different from that of her own family and muses about how "hard times" influenced her family.

Then there were Pete and Matt. They were bachelors and cousins of Dad's from both sides of his family. They lived in a "house" down by the river. By "house" I mean a large cave dug into the riverbank, with a roof over it, chimney and all. There was nothing else like that in our community, and they became quite famous. Pete was particularly clever with his hands, and head, too, even to the point of composing good poetry. With his great sense of humour he was welcome wherever they went and at home with everyone. We loved their visits, and they always went home with a jar of cream or a pat of homemade butter. Matt just sat there laughing and puffing away at his pipe. If you asked him how he was, he always replied, "Oh, still in the land of the living." It is good to remember old friends.

I wish I could, just for once, go again to fetch the cows that pastured in the coulee a mile away from home. The main attractions were the wild violets and cowslips that grew in the marsh. Childhood memories are so clear. When summer and autumn came to an end and signs of winter appeared, it seemed unbearable to us kids waiting for the big Eaton's parcel, coming with clothes to see us through the winter. Then came getting our parts for the Christmas concert and so the yearly cycle came to an end, only to begin all over again. We had been provided for all through the year, as promised.

Life was simple, hard, and satisfying through those years in the thirties. Methinks we are none the worse—indeed, we might even be the better for it.

Helen Wall writes about her parents, John and Anna Hiebert, who lived in Altona, Manitoba. With ingenuity and a bit of elbow grease, her father managed to get better living quarters for his family.

We had only a small house, and it was very crowded because at that time we were a family of six children. Dad fattened seven steers and sold them for $50 each. He bought the Queens Hotel in Plum Coulee for $350 with the steer money, as the hotel had to be torn down. Since it was thirteen miles away from our place, we went for months with horses and wagons to bring all the wood back to our farm. Then all the wood was sorted out and we had our house built—seven rooms, two storeys. We moved into it in November 1933, and that was one of my best days. Our walls might have included two or three different colours of paint, but we were happy that we all had room.

My mother always raised turkeys and ducks for Christmas money. That year it went to buy seven new windows. We got very small gifts but having the new house made up for that.

Alder A. Cranton now lives in Craigmyle, Alberta. He writes that although they had many happy times in the 1930s, this is his favourite memory.

Our family of Mom, Dad, and four boys saw many hardships and sorrows in the thirties. We lost our house by fire in 1929, so going into the 1930s must have been heartbreaking for our parents. However, there were happy times, too.

In 1934 my brother Harland, who was fourteen at the time and somewhat of an artist, was determined to help us have a happy Christmas. Although he never saw the ocean, he loved ships and pirates and all the excitement that went along with the high seas. He decided to try to draw a sort of comic strip and have it published in the Calgary *Herald*. He didn't know that his work could not be used in serial form, but three shots of his creation were published, much to the pride of his family and friends.

A wonderful group in Calgary called "The Sunshine

Club" stepped in and sent out a parcel to our family. I remember so plainly one of our neighbours coming from town with team and sleigh and stopping to deliver this parcel. It was quite a big box and was loaded with gifts for all of us.

What a Christmas that was. I think nearly everything was second-hand but that didn't make the slightest difference to us.

Harland got paper, paints, and everything he needed to pursue his love of art work. I remember that my favourite picture of the ones he painted was of a tired traveller sitting at his gate. Harland called it "Home at Last."

The rest of us got toys, books, and other useful items. I got a real metal toy car, and we got a colouring book that had been done, but we cherished it and I still have it to this day. It was called "Tom Kitten's Painting Book." I can't remember everything that was in the parcel, but it was the nicest gift anyone could have received. Charities like "Sunshine" must have given many poor children a Merry Christmas in those terrible times.

Eileen Hamilton, who lives in Moose Jaw, was the daughter of a small-town CPR agent. When I asked her for happy memories, at first she was hard put to remember anything sunny or funny about those days, but then she remembered the excitement of an electrical storm.

Everything was dry as dust and it was a storm. Big electrical balls of fire were shooting off the wires in Dad's office, and grain doors (from the grain cars waiting to be filled) were being tossed into our station windows just like someone was shuffling playing cards. It was raining grain doors and glass. Mum and Dad were trying to put up blankets to protect us when we insisted on watching the "show" rather than do as we were told and go up to our bedroom and crawl under the bed.

Children of the depression often have fond memories of those days. Their parents tended to shield them from the harsh realities as much as possible. But, in one way or another, the hard times left their mark on everyone who lived through them. *Eileen Comstock*

Eileen also remembers pure white twin baby calves born at sunrise on Easter Sunday morning. She says that is etched in her mind and heart as one being blessing another sans dust.

Yvonne Reimer remembers their district in Winnipeg, Manitoba, as being neighbourly.

Neighbours were really neighbours in those days. There was little moving and so everyone knew everybody. Anyone had any trouble; they could count on a neighbour's help. There was an empty field across the street from our house, and one evening three or four of us kids were playing cricket. Gradually more and more folks from the houses around came out to play, and we ended up playing baseball with full teams instead.

There were another two empty lots next to our place. Dad bought the $1 permission to use the lots as a garden. His friend the farmer, whom he sometimes worked for, came in with a horse and plough and turned the sod over. Then Dad and the bigger boys forked it over until it was smooth. Mom planted the little seeds, and we all helped plant potatoes. I loved eating peas straight from the plant and pulling up the little carrots to munch on. If I ever went missing Mom knew where to find me. I was probably sleeping between the rows of corn.

John J. Molgat, who grew up in the Interlake District of Manitoba, finds pleasure in remembering the unfolding of the seasons as it affected the pursuit of the diversions of young people, very young men in particular.

As winter drew to a close there was an annual contest at the school as to who would announce the sighting of the first reliable harbinger of spring—the crow. There were no ravens around in those days so a large black bird had to be a crow just returned from the far South, and conclusive evidence that winter was at an end. The only point of dispute was about the veracity of the witness—it had to be a boy as nobody in his right mind would believe a girl—and hearsay or second-hand testimony such as "My father—brother—sister or whatever saw a crow this morning" was totally inadmissible.

To everything there is a season, and early spring when small patches of the schoolyard became snow-free and dry was "marble time." At school recess, contestants in the game would be squatting in circles under the warming sun. This was in the depths of the Great Depression, and we gambled only with the common baked clay marbles that could be bought fifty or more in a 5-cent mesh bag. Their drawback was that they were very friable and your capital as well as your winnings would quickly disintegrate into powder if kept in your pocket. A prized possession was a coloured glass or "alley" or a large ball bearing. If each of the other participants in the game owned one, you could by mutual consent declare that your "alley" was your "shooter" only, hence could not be won by your opponent.

And one day, suddenly and inexplicably, marble time was over; all marbles disappeared and nobody even suggested playing any more. It was baseball—or rather in the school-yard, softball or slowball time. If there weren't enough players to form opposing teams, we had a game for which I cannot recall the English term (all of us spoke French)—we called it for some totally obscure reason "jouer a la vache." Runs were only to first base and back to home plate. You remained at bat until struck or tagged out, then were relegated to outfield to work your way back to bat by stages from fielder to baseman to pitcher to catcher as successive batters lost their turn. And then, with the last day of school, baseball also came to an end.

Beatrix Dunn writes from Winnipeg, Manitoba, about her family's arrival from England in 1930, just in time to have to cope with the depression.

Our family arrived in Winnipeg from Sussex, England, in 1930 to join relatives who had settled here several years earlier. The family consisted of my grandparents, my mother, two sisters, and myself. We had grown up with music and dancing, and when sister Joyce was sixteen she opened her own dancing school. At first it was held every Saturday morning and some evenings for private lessons—in our living room. Joyce was still in school at the time. She charged 25 cents a lesson. Mother was a great help in playing the piano. When we decided to stage a recital, Mother designed and made most of the costumes as well. Our first recital was held in the Glenwood School gymnasium in St. Vital, and the gym was packed—mostly by proud parents and relatives, I suspect. Because of the recital, the manager of the Onyx Theatre asked Joyce if some of her pupils would perform between shows. That was so successful that the audience couldn't be accommodated and the show had to be continued on following nights. Joyce taught for several years and gave much to her pupils and the community. Once we hired a bus and travelled to Dominion City to perform at a country fair. Finally, we were able to hire a band to accompany the children as they performed, and two years later Joyce married the band leader and gave up the dancing school. I will always remember the exciting times we had, and those memories wipe away memories of hardships we had to endure.

Furrows and Faith, the local history book of Mossbank, Saskatchewan, and surrounding area, records small rays of sunshine from districts in the area.

Leora Curtis recalls how much the Wiltse family enjoyed the fellowship in the Ford district. They always had such pleasant memories of the social evenings at the school. One delightful event occurred when the Wiltses celebrated their 25th wedding anniversary on January 2, 1937. It was a bitterly cold night, but all the neighbours and Ford friends came in sleigh-loads to give them a surprise party.

Ruth Davis of Mossbank contributed the story about an unusual gift, and her final message sums up the sentiments of many of us "children of the thirties."

An Ardill district bachelor, blacksmith, pianist, and very unique character by the name of Tom Conlan had the misfortune to have his prized old Buick coupe burned beyond use. On the occasion of a community-planned 25th wedding anniversary, he appeared with his own original gift, a long-handled dustpan. How appropriate for those days! Along with this dustpan, he presented his personal greetings or wishes, written in beautiful English script on a shiny and silky smooth metal valentine. (The occasion was February 13, 1931.) The inscription went thus:

> Knives, forks, spoons and all the rest
> I hope that you'll like this the best.
> A souvenir of an old friend
> Burned too badly to mend.

A part of a coupe
Made into a scoop
And the handle so long that you won't have to stoop!

Ruth contemplated the years of the thirties with wry affection.

Personally, I can only reflect on my "growing years" in the thirties with a deep feeling of gratitude for having been a child of that era. The qualities that shone forth in my parents I can only hope are inherent. Certainly, there was a decided lack of money and, as a result, hardship and deprivations. Yet as children, we were often unaware. In our home there was an adult expression: "Little pitchers have big ears." I disliked the expression intensely as it inferred that we, as children, were not to be "in" on discussion and topics of real concern to the adult. But as a result, those childhood years were comparatively carefree and happy, though we were not completely ignorant of the scene set by the elements. Should a ledger of lasting impressions be set up, I could only list those of the child as "assets." The parents suffered the liabilities. (Courtesy of the editor, Phyllis Zado)

EPILOGUE

Ruth Davis's tribute to parents in the hard times says that the parents had the liabilities, the children the assets. That was the generation gap of the thirties. We, the children of the thirties, were certainly moulded, for better and for worse, by the Great Depression.

We were afraid of debt. Most of us would be wealthier today if we had had the boldness to borrow, expand, and grow. Instead we opted for slow and steady—pay as you go. I am not sure that was entirely a liability. Few of us are millionaires, but even fewer went bankrupt.

We are openhanded and have passed the trait on to our progeny. Not only do we support organized charities, but also, if you hear of a fire that destroys a home or someone hurt so badly that he cannot work or a child that needs an operation at Sick Kids way down in Toronto, the next thing you hear is that a benefit is being organized by neighbours to come to their aid.

One of our most visible traits is our inability to throw away things. We laugh about it and long for uncluttered closets and empty drawers, or even a shed with room enough left to store the lawn mower. It is a vain hope. Our mind set was petrified long ago when our dads saved tobacco cans to store stove bolts, rusty staples, and stray washers, and our mothers cut buttons off raggedy underwear and saved the leg-backs of old pants to use as patches on the knees of the next pair.

We are trusting. To the point of stupidity. Our age group falls for re-roofing and other home improvement scams, for fake charities and phone solicitations. We just can't seem to bring ourselves to believe that anyone is out to cheat us. It is only after a lot of lectures from our kids, or actually becoming victims, that most of us have learned to lock our doors.

We may believe in the "goodness of man" but that trust does

not extend to government—especially any government farther away than the local municipal council, and even they had better keep their noses clean. The stock market ranks right up there with nuclear physics—both are remote and dangerous to mess around with. We really trust neither the railroads nor the banks. They are out to get us if they can. (Besides, there is a lot to say for a little stash of ready cash under the mattress, too.) And as for multinationals—well!

We have the "work ethic" and a lot of us don't know how to let go of it. We are so used to judging and being judged by what work we do and how well we do it that having to quit work seems more like a sentence of death than a licence to enjoy retirement. For many of us, work—accomplishing something worthwhile—is our pleasure. The idea of living in retirement, waking each morning to ask, "What will I play at today?" is nothing to look forward to. We need to extend our boundaries, to learn that there are other possibilities.

Actually, we are what the depression and the trials of the hard times made us. We lived through them and emerged with memories imprinted on our characters. We are the products of the depression, and we survived. Sometimes—in those years when gloom and pessimism seemed the rational response—sometimes—many times—the sun shone through.

We remember.